PHOTOSHOP 5

in easy steps

Robert Shufflebotham

COMPUTER STEP

In easy steps is an imprint of Computer Step
Southfield Road . Southam
Warwickshire CV33 OFB . England

Tel: 01926 817999 Fax: 01926 817005
http://www.computerstep.com

Notice of Liability

Every effort has been made to ensure that this book contains accurate
and current information. However, Computer Step and the author shall
not be liable for any loss or damage suffered by readers as a result of
any information contained herein.

Trademarks

Photoshop®, Illustrator®, PageMaker® and PostScript® are registered
trademarks of Adobe Systems Incorporated. All other trademarks are
acknowledged as belonging to their respective companies.

Printed and bound in the United Kingdom

ISBN 1-84078-049-5

Contents

Basic Theory

An understanding of the basics of colour is important if you are to get the best out of Photoshop. Refer back to this section from time to time. As your understanding of Photoshop grows, so will your appreciation of the concepts of colour that underpin the whole process of image capture and image manipulation.

This section also covers RGB, CMYK and Greyscale setup options and monitor calibration.

Covers

Chapter One

Bitmaps and Vectors

Photoshop is an image-editing application with a wealth of tools and commands for working on digital images or bitmaps. There are utilities for retouching, colour correcting, compositing and more. There are also over 90 functional and creative filters that can be applied to entire images, or selected areas within images.

A bitmap image consists of a rectangular grid, or raster, of pixels – in concept, very much like a mosaic. When you edit a bitmap you are editing the colour values of individual pixels or groups of pixels.

Image-editing applications differ fundamentally from vector-based applications such as Adobe Illustrator and Macromedia FreeHand. In these applications, you work with objects that can be moved, scaled, transformed, stacked and deleted as individual or grouped objects, but all the time each exists as a complete, separate object.

These applications are called vector drawing packages, as each object is defined by a mathematical formula. Because of this, they are resolution-independent – you can scale vector drawings up or down (either in the originating application or in a page layout application such as QuarkXPress or Adobe PageMaker) and they will still print smoothly and crisply.

You should always try to scan an image at, or slightly larger than, the size at which you intend to use it. This means you will avoid having to increase the size of the image.

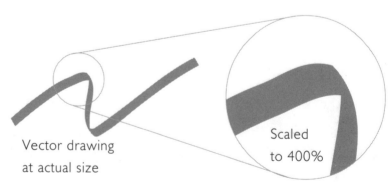

Vector drawing
at actual size

Scaled
to 400%

In contrast, bitmaps are created at a set resolution – a fixed number of pixels per inch. If you scan an image at a specific resolution, then double its size, you are effectively halving its resolution (unless you add more pixels). You are likely to end up with a blocky, jagged image, as you have increased the size of the individual pixels that make up the bitmap image.

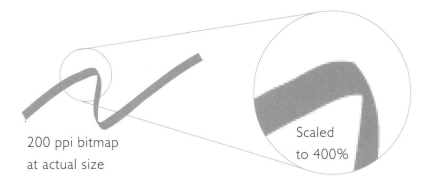

200 ppi bitmap
at actual size

Scaled
to 400%

Bitmaps and Bit-depth

An important factor when the digital data for an image is captured, typically at the scanning stage, is its bit-depth. Bit-depth refers to the amount of digital storage space used to record information about the colour of a pixel. The more bits you use, the more colour information you can store to describe the colour of a pixel – but also, the larger the file size you end up with.

More, rather than less, colour information is usually desirable, as this means the image can represent more shades of colour, with finer transitions between colours and greater density of colour, leading to a more realistic image.

To output realistic images using PostScript technology an image should be able to represent 256 grey levels. A 24-bit scan is sufficient for recording 256 grey levels for each of the Red, Green and Blue channels, resulting in a possible combination of over 16 million colours.

Ideally, when you work on images in Photoshop you will do so using a 24-bit monitor capable of displaying over 16 million colours. This ensures that you see all the colour detail in the image. Although you can work on images using only thousands of colours, for best results, especially where colour reproduction is important, you need to work with as many colours as possible.

Pixels and Resolution

Pixels

A pixel is the smallest element in a bitmap image such as a scan. Pixel is short for 'picture element'. Zoom in on an image in Photoshop and you will start to see the individual pixels – the fundamental building blocks – that make up the image. When working in Photoshop, you are editing pixels, changing their colour, shade and brightness.

Resolution

A key factor when working on bitmap images is resolution. This is measured in pixels per inch (ppi).

Pixels can vary in size. If you have an image with a resolution of 100 ppi, each pixel would be 1/100th of an inch square. In an image with a resolution of 300 ppi, each pixel would be 1/300th of an inch square – giving a much finer, less blocky result.

Printer resolution measured in dots per inch (dpi) is not the same as image resolution measured in pixels per inch (ppi). Printer dots are a fixed size, pixels can vary in size.

When working on images that will eventually be printed on a printing press, you need to work on high-resolution images. These are scanned images whose resolution is twice the halftone screen frequency (measured in lines per inch – lpi) that will be used for final output – that is when you output to bromide or film.

For example, for a final output screen frequency of 150 lpi – a typical screen frequency used for glossy magazines – you need to scan your image at a resolution of 300 ppi.

Resolutions of double the screen frequency are important for images with fine lines, repeating patterns or textures. You can achieve acceptable results, especially when printing at screen frequencies greater than 133 lpi, using resolutions of 1½ times the final screen frequency.

Images intended for multimedia presentations or the World Wide Web need only be 72 ppi, which is effectively the screen resolution.

To work with images for positional purposes only, as long as you can get accurate enough on-screen results and laser proofs, you can work with much lower resolutions.

RGB and CMYK Colour Models

As you start working with Adobe Photoshop there are two colour models that you need to be aware of. These are the RGB (Red, Green, Blue) and CMYK (Cyan, Magenta, Yellow and BlacK) colour models.

RGB is important because it mirrors the way the human eye perceives colour. It is the model used by scanners and digital cameras to capture colour information in digital format, and it is the way that your computer monitor describes colour.

Red, green and blue are referred to as the **additive primaries**. You can add varying proportions of the three colours to produce millions of different colours – but still a more limited range (or 'gamut') than in nature, due to the limitations of the phosphor screen coating of the monitor. If you add 100% red, green and blue light together, you get white. You produce the **secondary** colours when you add red and blue to get magenta; green and blue to get cyan; red and green to get yellow.

The CMYK colour model is referred to as the **subtractive** colour model. It is important because this is the colour model used by printing presses.

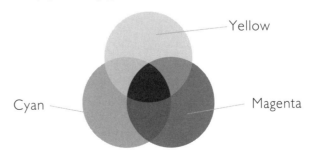

If you subtract all cyan, magenta and yellow when printing you end up with the complete absence of colour – white.

On the printing press, cyan, magenta, yellow and black are combined to simulate a huge variety of colours. Printers add black because, although in theory, if you combine 100% each of cyan, magenta and yellow you produce black, in reality, because of impurities in the dyes, you only get a muddy brown.

Colour Gamuts

Colour gamut refers to the range of colours that a specific device is capable of producing. There are millions of colours in the visible spectrum that the eye can discern. Scanners, monitors and printing presses cannot reproduce every colour in the visible spectrum – the range of colours they are capable of producing is their gamut.

From the desktop publishing point of view, the process of capturing digital colour information, viewing and manipulating this on-screen and then finally printing the image using coloured inks is complicated, because the gamut of a colour monitor is different to the gamut of CMYK and Pantone inks.

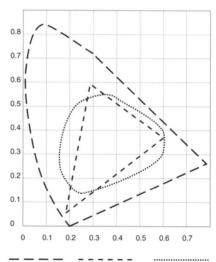

Visible Spectrum   Monitor   SWOP-CMYK

...cont'd

There are colours (especially vibrant yellows and deep blues) that can be displayed on a monitor but cannot be printed using traditional CMYK inks.

Typically, when you work in Photoshop, you will work in RGB (Red, Green, Blue) mode. RGB mode is faster to work in than CMYK mode, and in RGB mode all Photoshop options and commands are available to you. When you have finished making necessary adjustments and corrections to the image, you will need to convert it to CMYK mode, before saving/exporting the image in EPS or TIFF format for use in a page layout application such as Adobe PageMaker or QuarkXPress.

When you convert from RGB to CMYK mode, Photoshop converts out-of-gamut colours (in this case, colours that can be seen on screen, but not printed) into their nearest printable equivalent.

RGB Setup

RGB setup allows you to define a device-independent colour space in which to work. In previous versions of Adobe Photoshop, the RGB working space was that of the monitor. When images were viewed on different monitors the results could prove unpredictable.

 When you choose an option from the RGB pop-up, the Gamma, White Point and Primaries change automatically. Don't change these settings unless you have considerable knowledge and experience of colour printing.

To set the RGB workspace, choose File > Colour Settings > RGB Setup. Choose an RGB workspace for your image from the RGB pop-up.

Sticking with the default colour space (sRGB) is a safe bet if you are new to colour management and it is not your main concern at the outset, or if you are working with images intended for the Web or multimedia. Choose Apple RGB if you want to use the same RGB colour space that previous versions of

Adobe Photoshop used as a default. ColorMatch RGB (based on the Radius PressView display) is commonly regarded as a good choice for professional publishers as it comes closest to matching the range of colours that can typically be reproduced in print and displayed on monitors.

 It is important that anyone else viewing the same image does so on a correctly calibrated monitor and using the same RGB workspace if colours are to be viewed accurately and consistently on different monitors.

2 Select the Display Using Monitor Compensation option so that when you open an image it is converted to your monitor's RGB colour space for the current work session.

CMYK Setup

CMYK Setup options are important to ensure correct and predictable results when you convert RGB images to CMYK for print. Use the Built-in option if you are an experienced Photoshop user and familiar with the options available, or if you have been told by your commercial printer the appropriate settings to use. If you are new to Photoshop and colour management, the ICC option is probably the best choice.

An ICC (International Colour Consortium) profile defines the colour space for a specific device (eg, a printer or a monitor).

Profiles are stored in System\Preferences\ColorSync Profiles (Mac), Windows\System\Colour folder (Windows). You may have to obtain the correct profiles before you can select them. Try www.apple.com/colorsync or www.microsoft.com/hwtest/hcl/ as starting points for locating appropriate printer profiles. Alternatively, try the web site of the printer manufacturer.

1 To set CMYK options choose File > Colour Settings > CMYK Setup. Click the ICC options at the top of the CMYK Setup dialogue box.

2 Use the Profile pop-up to choose the profile of the actual printer you will be using.

If you are using an RGB printer (eg, a low end inkjet printer) there is no need to enter CMYK setup information.

Adobe has a useful section at its Website which deals in more detail with Photoshop version 5's colour management options: www.adobe.com/ supportservice/ custsupport/ TECHGUIDE/ PSHOP/main.html

3 Choose a Colour Management Module (CMM) from the Engine pop-up. The CMM is the software colour management

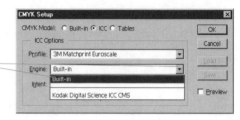

module that brings the various ICC colour profiles together and manages colour to ensure device independent colour management. Built-in refers to the Adobe Photoshop built-in CMM and is a good choice for beginners.

4 Leave the Intent pop-up on Perceptual. This option preserves the original relationships from colour to colour and achieves the most natural result.

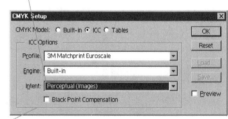

5 Leave the Black Point Compensation option unchecked.

6 Click the Preview option to see the results of your selections in any open image windows.

Greyscale Setup

If you are working with greyscale images you need to decide how the image will be treated.

Dot Gain refers to the expected increase in size of a halftone dot (between film and final output) caused by the spread of ink as it is absorbed by paper.

1 To set Greyscale options, choose File > Colour Settings > Greyscale Setup.

2 Select the RGB option if your images are intended for the World Wide Web or multimedia use. The RGB option creates a composite grey which consists of equal amounts of red, green and blue light. There is no compensation for dot gain when you use this setting.

3 Choose Black Ink if your images will be printed. The Black Ink setting is based on the settings in the CMYK Setup dialogue box. The greys in the image behave like the black plate in a CMYK image. This option includes compensation for dot gain.

4 Select the Preview option if you have an image open and you want to see how the different settings affect the image.

Monitor Calibration

It is important to calibrate your monitor so that colours in your image are displayed accurately. Calibrating your monitor should eliminate any colour casts (typically reddish or blueish) on your monitor and ensure that the monitor displays greys as neutrally as possible.

For monitor calibration to be effective, you should not adjust the brightness and contrast settings on your monitor after you have completed the calibration process, and you must ensure that the lighting conditions within the room remain constant.

Use the Adobe Gamma utility to calibrate the monitor you are using and to define the RGB colour space that your monitor can display.

Once you have calibrated your monitor, Photoshop can compensate for the differences between the colour space in which your image resides and the colour space of the monitor you are using.

The Adobe Gamma utility enables you to calibrate the contrast and brightness, gamma (midtones), colour balance and the white point of the monitor. Calibration settings that you create are saved as an ICC (International Colour Consortium) profile with a .icm extension.

Use the Adobe Gamma Wizard if you are do not have previous experience of calibrating a monitor.

1 (Windows) Choose Settings > Control Panel from the Start Menu. Double-click the Adobe Gamma icon to display the dialog.
(Macintosh) Use the Apple menu to choose Control Panel > Adobe Gamma.

2 Choose Step by Step Wizard, then click the Next button.

...cont'd

Leave your monitor turned on for at least 30 minutes before you calibrate. This allows the phosphors time to warm up fully and for the display to stabilise.

3 Click the Load button to choose a monitor profile which matches the monitor you are using most closely. (Windows) Profiles are stored in the Windows\ System\ Colour folder. (Mac) Profiles are stored in the System\Preferences\ColorSync Profiles folder. Profiles should be available from your monitor manufacturer's Web site, or you can try: www.microsoft.com/hwtest/hcl/. Click the Next button.

4 Adjust the Brightness and Contrast settings of your monitor. Refer to the monitor handbook if you are unsure of how to adjust these settings. Click the Next button.

5 Only change the Phosphors pop-up if you know that your monitor's phosphors are different from the default selection. Click the Next button.

6 With the View Single Gamma Only option selected, drag the
Gamma slider until the square in the middle of the patterned
lines fades, as far as possible,
into the pattern. This
defines the brightness of the
midtones on your monitor.
(Un-focus your eyes slightly
to help achieve the correct
result.) Click the Next button.

7 For Desired Gamma choose a target gamma. This option is
not available on Windows systems which cannot control the
monitor. If you intend to prepare images for the World
Wide Web or multimedia presentations, choose a gamma of
2.2. If you intend to print images using CMYK inks, you
typically choose a gamma of 1.8. Click the Next button.

8 Leave the Hardware White
Point on the default setting
unless you know
this to be
inaccurate. Click
the Next button.

9 Leave Adjusted
White Point on
Same as
Hardware unless you want to view the image at a different
colour temperature to that set by the monitor's factory
specified setting. Click the Next button.

10 Click the Finish button to save settings as
an .icm compatible profile.

The Working Environment

This section covers the basics of the Photoshop working environment, getting you used to the Photoshop window, the Toolbox, palettes and a number of standard Photoshop conventions that you will find useful as you develop your Photoshop skills.

It also covers the basics of printing composite images to a PostScript laser printer as well as techniques for undoing commands as you work on your images.

Covers

Chapter Two

The Photoshop Screen Environment

There are three 'screen modes' to choose from when working on images in Photoshop. The screen mode icons are located at the bottom of the toolbox. Full screen with menu bar mode is useful when working on individual images because it clears away the clutter of the Finder environment (Mac) or the Windows desktop. Use Full screen mode to see the image without the distraction of other screen elements, and without any other colours interfering with the colours in your image.

Standard screen mode

Full screen
with menu bar
mode

Full screen mode

I Click this icon to return to Standard screen mode.

2 Click this icon to go to Full screen with menu bar mode.

3 Click this icon to go to Full screen mode. Press the Tab key to hide/show the toolbox and palettes.

...cont'd

Command (often referred to as 'Apple' on the Mac) and Ctrl (Windows), and alt (Mac) and Alt (Windows) are used identically as modifier keys. Shift is standard on both platforms.

Windows Environment

The Windows environment offers identical functionality to the Macintosh environment, as you can see from a comparison of the Windows and Macintosh screen shots.

Windows users can use the right mouse button to access context sensitive menus; Mac users can hold down the ctrl key and press their single mouse button.

The Image Window

You need the rulers showing to create ruler guides. Use the shortcut Command/Ctrl + R to show or hide rulers.

Close box

Rulers

Sizes bar

View Percentage

Title bar

Image

Scroll bars

Resize box

Using the Toolbox

There are a number of useful general techniques that relate to choosing tools in the Toolbox, including those from the expanded range of hidden tool pop-ups.

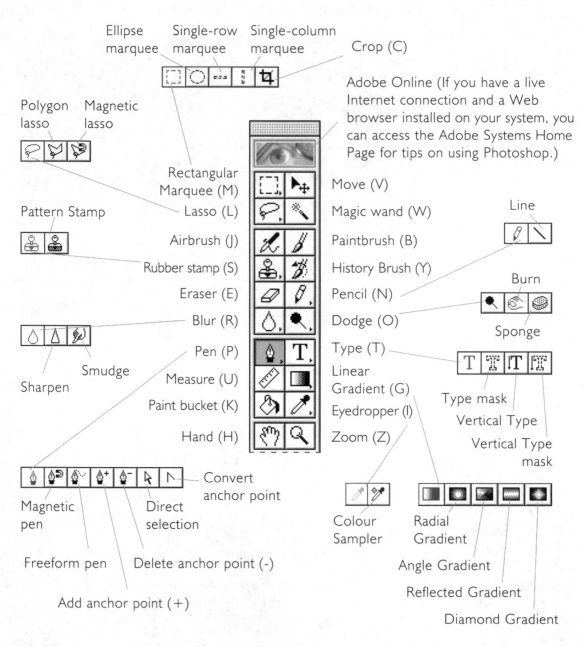

Ellipse marquee

Single-row marquee

Single-column marquee

Crop (C)

Adobe Online (If you have a live Internet connection and a Web browser installed on your system, you can access the Adobe Systems Home Page for tips on using Photoshop.)

Polygon lasso

Magnetic lasso

Rectangular Marquee (M)

Lasso (L)

Pattern Stamp

Airbrush (J)

Rubber stamp (S)

Eraser (E)

Blur (R)

Pen (P)

Measure (U)

Paint bucket (K)

Hand (H)

Sharpen

Smudge

Move (V)

Magic wand (W)

Paintbrush (B)

History Brush (Y)

Pencil (N)

Dodge (O)

Type (T)

Linear Gradient (G)

Eyedropper (I)

Zoom (Z)

Line

Burn

Sponge

Type mask

Vertical Type

Vertical Type mask

Magnetic pen

Freeform pen

Add anchor point (+)

Delete anchor point (-)

Direct selection

Convert anchor point

Colour Sampler

Radial Gradient

Angle Gradient

Reflected Gradient

Diamond Gradient

...cont'd

Foreground colour — Switch colours (X)

Default colours (D) — Background colour

Standard mode (Q) — Quick Mask mode (Q)

Standard screen mode (F) — Full screen mode (F)

Full screen mode with menu bar (F)

1 Press the keyboard shortcut (in brackets) to access tools.

2 Click and hold on any tool with a small triangle in the bottom right corner to see all tools in that tool group.

Double-click on a tool to show the appropriate Options palette for that tool.

3 Hold down alt/Alt and click on any tool in a tool group to cycle through the available tools. Alternatively, hold down Shift, then press the keyboard shortcut for that tool group a number of times. For example, press 'O' three times to cycle through all the tools in the Dodge tool group.

Use Display & Cursor Preferences in the File menu to change the default appearance of painting and other Cursors.

4 Press Tab to hide/show all palettes, including the toolbox. Hold down Shift, then press the Tab key to hide/show all palettes except the Toolbox.

5 Press Caps Lock to change painting cursors to a precise crosshair cursor, which indicates the centre of the painting tool. Press Caps Lock again to return to standard cursors.

Document and Scratch Sizes

The Sizes Bar is useful for monitoring disk space and memory considerations as you work on your images.

Document Sizes

With Document Sizes selected, you will see two numbers separated by a slash. The first number is the size of the image when all layers are flattened. The second number may be larger and represents the file storage size, whilst the image

contains additional layers and/or alpha channels you may have set up. In images that consist of only a single layer, with no additional channels, both numbers are the same.

Scratch Sizes

Use the Plug-ins & Scratch Disk preferences (File > Preferences) to specify the hard disk you want Photoshop to use as a Scratch disk.

The Scratch disk is an underlying technical detail that you should be aware of when using Photoshop. The Scratch disk is a designated hard disk that Photoshop utilises as 'virtual' memory if it runs out of memory (RAM) whilst working on one or more images.

With Scratch Sizes selected in the Sizes Bar you again see two numbers separated by a slash. The first number represents the

amount of memory (RAM) Photoshop needs to handle all currently open pictures. The second number represents the actual amount of memory available to Photoshop. When the first number is greater than the second, Photoshop is using the Scratch disk as virtual memory.

(Macintosh) Switch off Virtual Memory in the Memory control panel. Photoshop uses its own virtual memory management system to work with the Scratch disk.

As a general rule of thumb when working in Photoshop, you should have free disk space of at least 3–5 times the file size of the image you are working on. This is because Photoshop makes use of the Scratch disk as virtual memory and because Photoshop needs to hold more than one copy of the image you are working on for the Undo, Revert and From Saved commands.

Ruler Guides and Grids

You can show a grid in your image window to help with alignment and measuring, and you can also drag in ruler guides from the rulers. Both sets of guides are non-printing. You can customise the appearance of the grid and guides using File > Preferences > Guides & Grid.

Make sure that Snap to Guides is selected in the View menu if you want cursors and selections to snap to guides and the grid. This is very useful for aligning elements accurately.

 To hide or show the grid, choose View > Show / Hide Grid.

2 To create a ruler guide, first choose View > Show Rulers to display the rulers along the top and left edges of the image window. Position your cursor in a ruler and then click and drag onto your image to create either a vertical or horizontal guide.

Take care when repositioning ruler guides that you don't reposition the entire background layer accidentally. Make sure you see the bi-directional arrows which indicate that you are dragging a guide.

3 To reposition a ruler guide, select the Move tool, position your cursor on a guide, then click and drag. The cursor changes to a bi-directional arrow when you pick up a guide.

4 To remove a ruler guide, drag the ruler guide back into the ruler it came from. Alternatively, choose View > Clear Guides to remove all guides.

Moving Around

Use any combination of the Navigator palette, the Zoom tool, the Hand tool and the scroll bars for moving around and zooming in and out of your image.

1 Choose Window > Show Navigator to show the Navigator palette. In the palette, you can double-click the % entry box, enter a zoom % (0.198 – 1600%), then press Return/Enter. Alternatively,

drag the zoom slider to the right to zoom in, or to the left to zoom out. Each time you change your zoom level, the view in the Proxy Preview area updates.

Hold down Command/ Ctrl and the spacebar to temporarily access the zoom tool with any other tool selected. Add the Alt/Option key (Mac) or the Alt key (Windows) to the above combination to zoom out.

2 Drag the red box in the Proxy Preview area to move quickly to different areas of your image.

3 To use the Zoom tool, select it, position your cursor on the image and click to zoom in on the area around your cursor, in preset increments. With the Zoom tool selected, hold down alt/Alt. The cursor changes to the zoom out cursor; click to zoom out in the preset increments.

4 With the Zoom tool selected, you can also click and drag to define the area you want to zoom in on.

With any other tool selected, hold down the spacebar to temporarily access the hand tool.

5 You can use the Hand tool in addition to using the scroll bars to move around your image when you have zoomed in on it. Select the tool, position your cursor on the image, then click and drag to reposition.

The Info Palette

The Info palette (Window > Show Info) provides useful numerical read-outs relative to the position of the cursor on your image.

You can use it as an on-screen densitometer to examine colour values at the cursor. There are two colour read-outs. As a default, the first colour read-out is the actual colour under the cursor. For example, a read-out of red, green, and blue colour components in an RGB image. The default second read-out is for cyan, magenta, yellow and black values.

The palette also displays x and y coordinates, giving the precise location of the cursor as it moves over the image.

If you create a selection, there is a read-out of the width and height of the selection. The palette also displays values for some options such as rotating, skewing and scaling selections.

An exclamation mark next to the CMYK readouts indicates that a colour is out of gamut.

1 To change the default settings for the Info Palette, choose Palette Options from the pop-up menu.

2 Use the Mode pop-ups to choose the first and second colour read-outs.

3 You can also choose a unit of measurement for mouse coordinates.

Palette Techniques

There are eleven floating palettes in Photoshop. These movable palettes appear in front of images. Initially the palettes are grouped together. The default groupings for the palettes are Navigator-Info-Options, Colour-Swatches-Brushes, Layers-Channels-Paths-History-Actions.

1   You can show any of the palette groups by selecting the appropriate palette from the Window menu. To close a palette, click on the Close box (Mac) or Close icon (Windows) in the title bar of each palette.

This page uses Macintosh and Windows screen shots to illustrate the degree of similarity in functionality between the Windows and Macintosh platforms.

2   To move a palette, simply position your cursor in the title bar, then click and drag.

3   To choose a particular palette, click on the appropriate tab just below the title bar. You can drag these tabs to create separate palettes. Alternatively, you can drag a tab into another palette to create your own custom groupings of palettes.

4   You can shrink or roll up palettes to make the most of your available screen space. Click the Zoom box (Mac) or Minimise icon (Windows) in the title bar of the palette. Repeat the procedure to restore the palette to its original size. (You have to click twice on the Zoom/Minimise icon if the palette has been resized.)

5 You can use standard Macintosh and Windows techniques to resize the Swatches and Brushes, Navigator, Layers, Channels, Actions and Paths palettes by dragging.

6 You can collapse some of the palettes to show title bar and tabs only, by double-clicking a tab. Repeat the procedure to restore the palette to its original size.

7 Press the Tab key to hide/show all palettes including the toolbox. Hold down Shift, then press Tab to hide/show currently visible palettes, with the exception of the toolbox.

8 You can restore the default settings for a tool by choosing Reset Tool from the pop-up menu in the tool options palette. Choose Reset All Tools to restore default settings for all tools.

9 All palettes have a pop-up menu for accessing a range of commands or options relevant to the palette. Click and hold on the triangle (Mac), or just click the triangle (Windows).

Saving and Loading Custom Settings

When you save settings, you are creating an independent file which stores the custom information.

The Swatches, Brushes and Actions palettes, along with dialogue boxes, such as Duotones, Levels and Curves, have Save and Load options which allow you to save custom settings made in the palette or dialogue box and then load them into the same image, or into other Photoshop images. The following example is for the Brushes palette.

It's a good idea to set up a folder within your Adobe folder, or any other appropriate location, for saving your own custom settings. This means you will always be able to access and load the settings quickly and conveniently whenever you need them.

1   When you have customised the Brushes palette (see pages 72–73 and 84), choose Save Brushes in the pop-up menu (in a dialogue box, click the Save button) to save the changes.

2   The Save Brushes In dialogue box prompts you for a file name and location in which to save the settings.

3   To load previously saved settings, choose Replace Brushes/Load Brushes in the pop-up (in a dialogue box click the Load Button), then specify the location of the settings you previously saved. Click on the name, then click Open. Load Brushes adds the new brushes to the existing brushes in the palette. Replace Brushes replaces the current brushes with the new set.

Look in the Goodies folder, within the Adobe folder, for palettes that come with Photoshop. Try the Assorted Brushes as a starting point for experimenting with brush types.

4   Choose Reset Brushes in the pop-up menu to restore settings to their original defaults.

Printing Composites – Mac

A composite image is an image which has not been colour separated and can be useful for low-cost, basic proofing purposes. In a black-and-white laser printer composite, you get a complete image on one sheet of paper, with all colour values converted to shades of grey.

 The appearance of the Page Setup dialogue box varies according to the printer selected. Non-PostScript printers do not offer a complete set of options.

Page Setup

1 To print a composite image, first use the Chooser to select the printer you want to print to.

2 Choose File > Page Setup. Make sure the correct printer is selected from the 'Format for' pop-up. From the Paper pop-up, choose the actual physical size of the paper in your printer onto which you want to print. You can enter a Scale % entry box to increase/decrease the size of the image that prints. Use the Orientation buttons to control the orientation of the image.

3 Choose Adobe Photoshop 5 from the pop-up to specify Photoshop print options. Click the Screen button to change the size, angle and shape of the halftone screen dots. This can be useful for creating special effects. Click the Transfer button to map brightness values in an image to different shades when printed. Background and Border are useful when printing slides. Use Bleed to print outside the 'imageable' area of the page when outputting to an imagesetter.

4 Choose PostScript Options from the pop-up to set further PostScript options if required.

BEWARE

Choose File > Image Info and enter a caption if you want a caption to print with the image.

Printing the image

Choose File > Print. With General selected, make sure you have the correct printer chosen in the Printer pop-up. Enter the number of copies you want to print.

2 Choose Adobe Photoshop 5 from the pop-up. Check that encoding is set to Binary. This is a more compact and quicker format for sending image data than ASCII. Make sure that Space is set to Greyscale. Click the Print button when you are satisfied with the settings.

Registration Marks

Centre Crop Marks

Corner Crop Marks

Calibration Bars

This is the caption I wrote

Printing Composites – Windows

A composite image is an image which has not been colour separated and can be useful for low-cost, basic proofing purposes. In a black and white laser printer composite, you get a complete image, with all colour values converted to shades of grey.

1   To print a composite proof, choose File > Page Setup. Select the printer you want to print to. Check that Paper Size and Orientation are correct. Click the check boxes for calibration bars and registration marks as required. OK the dialogue box.

HOT TIP **You can choose File > Print, then click the Setup button to go into the Page Setup Dialogue box.**

2   Choose File > Print. Select the Print As and Encoding options, then click OK. (Binary encoding is a quick, efficient method of encoding image data; ASCII encoding results in a larger, plain-text file, but offers greater compatibility when moving files to and from the Windows platform. JPEG can only be used with PostScript Level 2 printers.)

The History Palette

Every time you modify your image this is recorded in the History palette as a history state. The History palette records the last 20 states of the image.

Once you close an image, all recorded history states and snapshots are discarded.

Use the History palette to return to a previous state of the image within the current work session. The most recent state of the image appears at the bottom of the list in the palette. Each state indicates the name of the tool or command used on the image.

| To return to a previous state of the image, make sure that the History palette is showing.

You can still use Edit > Undo to undo the last operation. In effect this steps you back one state in the History palette.

2 Click on a state in the History palette. The image reverts to that stage of the work session. States after the state you click on are dimmed. These subsequent states will be discarded if you continue to work from the selected state.

Use File > Revert to revert to the state of your image as it was when you last did a File > Save. The History palette is cleared of all previous history states when you use the Revert command.

3 Alternatively, drag the state slider up or down to indicate the state you wish to move to. Or, choose Step Forward/Step Backward from the pop-up menu in the History palette to move sequentially through the states. You can also use the keyboard shortcuts Command/Ctrl+Shift+Z to move to the next state. Use alt/Alt+Shift+Z to move to the previous state.

Deleting, Clearing & Purging States

There are three essential techniques for controlling the states listed in the History palette.

 Both techniques for deleting states delete the selected state and all states that occur after it. In other words, you are reverting to the state of the image previous to the state you delete.

Deleting States

You can delete states from the History palette to remove the changes to the image recorded by that state and all subsequent states.

1. To delete a history state, click on the name of the state, then choose Delete from the pop-up menu in the History palette.

2. Alternatively, drag the state into the Wastebasket icon at the bottom of the palette.

Clearing States

Clearing states leaves the image at its current state, but removes all previous states from the History palette.

1. To clear the History palette, use the pop-up menu to choose Clear History. All recorded states are deleted from the History palette, leaving the image at its most recent state.

Purging States

Purging states is useful if you get a low memory message. This is typically because the Undo buffer is becoming full with the changes to the image that it is having to record. When you purge states they are deleted from the Undo buffer, freeing up memory.

 You cannot undo the Purge states commands.

1. To purge states, hold down alt/Alt, then choose Clear History from the pop-up menu in the History palette. This command purges history states from the active image.

2. Choose Edit > Purge Histories if you want to purge all history states for all open images.

Taking Snapshots

By default the History palette records the result of the last 20 operations performed on an image. Older states of the image are automatically deleted. This keeps memory free for Photoshop. You can keep particular states of an image throughout a work session by taking a Snapshot of the image.

A Snapshot is created by default when you open an image. This appears at the top of the History palette.

| To create additional Snapshots, click on any state in the History palette.

2 Choose New Snapshot from the pop-up menu in the History palette. In the New Snapshot dialogue box enter a name. OK the dialogue box. A new Snapshot is added in the top section of the History palette.

Opening and Saving Files

Adobe Photoshop began life with the primary purpose of converting image formats for use on different applications and platforms. Since then it has gone on to become a market-leading image-editing application. This chapter covers the basic techniques of opening and saving images in Photoshop.

Covers

Chapter Three

Opening Images in Photoshop

Once you have launched Photoshop you can open images using the File menu. Some specialist file formats open using the File > Import command.

1   To open a picture from within Photoshop, choose File > Open. This takes you into the Open File dialogue box.

Click the Create button if it is available for Photoshop to create a thumbnail preview of the file you have selected in the file list box.

2   Navigate through folders and sub-folders as necessary to locate the file you wish to open, click on

the file name to select it, then click Open. Alternatively, just double-click the file name.

3   Use the Show Thumbnail option either to hide or to show the thumbnail area to the left of the dialogue box. Select the Show All Files option (Mac), or choose All Formats from the

Files of Type pop-up (Windows), to show all files in the selected folder.

Double-click Photoshop file icons in the Windows or Macintosh file-management environments to open the file. If Photoshop is not running, this will also launch Photoshop.

4   In Windows you can use the Open As command to open a file that has a missing or incorrect file extension. You can also choose from a list of the most recently opened files at the bottom of the File menu.

Scanning into Photoshop

You can scan into Photoshop either using the TWAIN interface, using a scanner plug-in designed for use with Photoshop, or, if your scanner does not have a plug-in for Photoshop, you can use the scanner software to scan the image, save the image in TIFF, PICT or BMP format, then open the file in Photoshop.

Make sure the plug-in for your scanner is in Photoshop's Import/Export plug-ins folder. Plug-in modules for installed scanners appear in the File > Import submenu.

1 The first time you scan into Photoshop using the TWAIN interface, choose File > Import > TWAIN Select. Locate your scanner, select the scanner icon and click OK to specify the scanner.

2 Choose File > Import > TWAIN Acquire. This takes you into your scanning software.

```
Anti-aliased PICT...
PICT Resource...
Quick Edit...
Twain Acquire...
Twain Select...
```

Refer to your scanning software manual for details of the controls available. Typically, you can choose settings for scan mode (greyscale, colour, line art etc.), resolution, scale, contrast, brightness and gamma settings.

Many of the scanning controls have equivalent functions in Photoshop. Scanning options vary from scanner to scanner, but you should be able to specify whether you are scanning a transparency or a photograph. The other essential decisions you need to make at this stage are mode, resolution and scale. You will also need to specify a crop area in the preview window.

Mode:	Gray-Scale
Original:	Reflective
Output:	200 ppi
Scale To:	100%
Range:	Automatic
Tone Curve:	Gamma 1.8
Descreen:	None
Sharpness:	None
Preferences:	General
Settings:	Current

If your scanner does not have a plug-in for Photoshop, use the scanner software to scan the image, save the image in TIFF, PICT or BMP format, then open it in Photoshop.

3 Click the scan button. Wait until the scanning process finishes and the image appears in an untitled Photoshop window. Save the image.

Opening Photo CD Images

Photo CD files are found inside the Images folder within the Photo CD folder.

The Photo CD format, developed by Kodak, and using the YCC colour model, is becoming a more and more popular method for creating and storing digital images. The YCC colour model provides an extremely broad range of colour. The Kodak Precision Color Management System (KPCMS) lets you control the colour mode and display of Photo CD images by specifying profiles for the source film and the destination output device.

The Kodak Precision Color Management System is automatically installed on your system when you install Photoshop.

1 To open a Photo CD Image, choose File > Open. Select the image you want to open and click OK. The Photo CD Plug-in dialogue box appears.

2 Use the Resolution pop-up menu to choose a resolution from 128 x 192 pixels (72k, 2.667 by 1.778 inches) to 2,048 x 3,072 pixels (18Mb, 42.668 by 28.445 inches). In this case, resolution refers to the dimensions of the image in pixels. All Photo CD images open in Photoshop at a resolution of 72 pixels per inch.

A product type of 052/55 denotes Universal Ektachrome, while 116/22 denotes Universal Kodachrome.

3 Click the Image Info button. The dialogue box gives information about the image and the medium of the original. Make a note of the medium of the original – whether it was a colour negative or slide (Colour Reversal). For a Colour Reversal, make a note of the 'Product Type of Original'. You will use this information in the Source option to select the appropriate Precision Transform for a specific Photo CD image. OK the Image Info box.

...cont'd

 Profiles are stored in System\ Preferences\ ColorSync Profiles folder (Mac); Windows\System \Colour folder (Windows). You may have to obtain the correct profiles before you can select them. (See page 15 for further information.)

4 Click the Source button. The folder in which ICC colour profiles are stored automatically opens. Make sure the Show Profile Attributes option is selected. Click on a profile to select it.

The attributes area at the bottom of the dialogue box will help you choose the correct profile according to the Product Type of Original you noted in the Image Info dialogue box. In this example the choice is Universal Ektachrome. If the Medium of Original is Colour Reversal, but you don't know the film type, use Universal Kodachrome. OK the dialogue box.

5 Click the Destination button. Select a profile for the output device. OK the dialogue box.

6 OK the Photo CD Plug-in dialogue box. The image will open in Photoshop.

Opening an EPS File

EPS files, which are created in applications such as Adobe Illustrator and Macromedia FreeHand, can contain object-oriented or 'vector' format information. When you open an EPS file in Photoshop, it is rasterized: that is, the vector information is converted into Photoshop's pixel-based format.

1 To open an EPS file as a new document, choose File > Open. Locate and highlight an EPS picture to be opened, then click the Open button. Alternatively, double-click the file name.

2 In the Rasterize dialogue box, choose a unit of measurement from the pop-up menus next to the height and width fields, and enter new dimensions if required.

3 Enter the resolution required for your final output device and choose an image mode from the Mode pop-up menu.

4 Select the Constrain Proportions box to keep the original proportions of the EPS. Select Anti-aliased to slightly blur pixels along edges to avoid unwanted jagged edges.

5 Click OK. The EPS appears in its own image window. It is now a bitmap image.

Placing an EPS File

You can also 'place' an Illustrator or FreeHand EPS file into an open Photoshop document.

 Before you place an EPS into Photoshop, it's a good idea to choose File > Preferences > General, then select the Anti-alias PostScript option. This preference helps create a smooth result.

1 To place an EPS file into an existing Photoshop file, first open a picture in Photoshop.

2 Choose File > Place. Use the Place Document dialogue box to specify the location and name of the EPS file, then click Place.

3 A bounding box with eight 'handles' and a cross through the placed image will appear on your Photoshop image. The EPS image itself may take a few seconds to draw inside the bounding box.

4 Drag a corner handle to resize the placed image. Hold down Shift as you drag to maintain proportions. Position your cursor inside the bounding box of the placed image and drag to reposition the image.

 If you don't want to accept the placed image, with the bounding box still visible, press the Esc key. If you have already placed the image you will have to delete the new layer. (See page 112.)

5 When you are satisfied, press Return/Enter, or double-click inside the bounding box. The rasterized file is placed on a new layer.

Saving Files

To create a thumbnail icon that will display in the thumbnail area of the Open dialogue box, choose File > Preferences > Saving Files. Select Always Save from the Image Previews pop-up, then click the Thumbnail option.

The basic principles of saving files in Photoshop – using 'Save' and 'Save As' – are the same as in any other Macintosh or Windows application. You should save regularly as you make changes to an image so that you do not lose changes you have made should a system crash occur. You should use Save As to save a new file in the first instance and to make copies of a file.

Photoshop supports numerous file formats for opening and saving images. Typically, you save an image in a particular format either to meet specific output or printing specifications, to compress the image to save disk space, or to open or import the image into an application that requires a particular file format.

To save an image in the first instance, choose File > Save As. Specify where you want to save the file. Enter a name for the file. Use the Format pop-up to choose an appropriate format. Click on the Save button.

To create image icons for the Finder on the Macintosh, choose File > Preferences > Saving Files. Select Always Save from the Image Previews pop-up, then click the Icon option.

2 To save changes that you have made to an image that you are working on, choose File > Save. The previously saved file is updated.

Photoshop Format

This is sometimes referred to as native format: use this format as you work on your image. Applications such as QuarkXPress will not import images in Photoshop format, but all of Photoshop's options, in particular layers, remain available to you when you save in this format. Photoshop also performs open and save routines more quickly when using its native format.

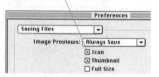

TIFF Format

TIFF (Tagged Image File Format), originally developed by Aldus, became a standard file format for scanned images in the early days of desktop publishing, and is common on both Mac and Windows platforms.

1 To save an image in TIFF format, choose File > Save As. The Save As dialogue box appears.

On the Macintosh, use the Saving Files preferences dialogue box to specify whether or not you want file extensions – e.g. '.tif' – automatically added when saving files.

2 Specify where you want to save the image and enter a name in the name entry box. Use the Format pop-up menu to choose TIFF, then click OK.

3 The TIFF options dialogue box will appear. Select Byte Order options and LZW Compression as required, then OK the dialogue box.

Byte Order

Use this option to specify whether you want the TIFF to be used on a Mac or a PC, as Mac and PC TIFF formats vary slightly.

LZW Compression

(Lempel-Ziv-Welch) is a compression format that looks for repeated elements in the computer code that describes the image and replaces these with shorter sequences. Most importantly, this is a 'lossless' compression scheme (i.e., none of the image's detail is lost). Applications such as QuarkXPress, Adobe PageMaker and Macromedia FreeHand can import TIFFs with LZW compression.

Photoshop EPS

EPS is generally more reliable for PostScript printing than TIFF file format, but generates file sizes which can be three to four times greater than TIFFs with LZW compression. To save in EPS format, do the following:

> Follow the procedure for saving TIFFs, but choose Photoshop EPS from the Format pop-up menu. Click OK. The EPS format dialogue box will appear. Specify your settings, then click OK.

Preview

This option specifies the quality of the low-resolution screen preview you see when you import the image into applications such as Adobe PageMaker and QuarkXPress. Use

'Macintosh (8bits/pixel)' for a colour preview. 'Macintosh (JPEG)' uses JPEG compression routines, but is only supported by Postscript Level 2 printers. Use TIFF if you want to use the image in Windows.

Encoding

Use binary encoding if you want to export the image for use with Adobe Illustrator. Some applications do not recognise binary encoding; in this case you have to use ASCII.

Clipping Path

Use the Path pop-up menu to select a path you have previously created in the image to become a clipping path. The clipping path acts as a mask on the EPS image when you import it into applications such as QuarkXPress and Adobe PageMaker. (See pages 146–147.)

Creating a New File

When you need a fresh, completely blank canvas to work on, you can create a new file.

Whilst the New dialogue box is active, if you have an image window already open, you can choose the window's name from the bottom of the Window menu; the New dialogue box will update with the settings from the file you selected.

1 To create a new file, choose File > New. Enter a name for the new document (or leave this as Untitled and do a Save As later).

2 Specify width and height settings. If you have copied or cut pixels to the clipboard, the width and height fields automatically reflect the dimensions of the elements on the clipboard.

3 Enter a resolution and choose a colour mode.

4 Select one of the contents options to specify the canvas background you want to begin with, then OK the dialogue box.

You can also use the Fill command to fill selections with colour.

5 To change the colour of the canvas, select a foreground colour (see Chapter Five, 'Defining Colours'). Next, choose Edit > Fill. Choose Foreground from the Use pop-up. Make sure Opacity is set to 100% and Mode is Normal. Click OK.

Getting Started with Images

There are a number of common techniques and tasks, such as cropping an image and making it larger or smaller, or changing the resolution to suit your final output needs, that you need to undertake on many of the images on which you work. This chapter covers a range of these tasks.

Covers

Chapter Four

Resampling Up

Resampling up involves interpolation. Interpolation is used when Photoshop has to add information – new pixels – that didn't previously exist to an image. There are three methods to choose from the pop-up in the Image size dialogue box. Bicubic gives best results, but takes longest; Nearest Neighbour is quickest, but least accurate.

When you resample up, new pixels are added to the image, so file size increases. Resampling takes place when you increase the resolution setting, or the width/height setting with the Resample Image option selected.

This example starts with a 2 in by 2 in image at 72 ppi.

1 Choose Image > Image Size. To keep the overall dimensions of the image, but increase the resolution, make sure that Resample Image is selected. Select Constrain Proportions so that the image's original proportions are maintained. Enter a higher value in the Resolution box.

To reset the dialogue box to its original settings, hold down alt/Alt, then click the Reset button.

2 The file size and total number of pixels increase, but the width and height dimensions remain the same.

...cont'd

You now have an image which is the same overall size, but which has more pixels in the same area, and therefore its resolution is increased:

When you resample an image, blurring may occur due to the process of interpolation. Use the Unsharp Mask filter to compensate for this. (See pages 169–170.)

3 To make the overall dimensions of the image bigger, but to keep the same resolution, again make sure that Resample Image is selected. Select Constrain Proportions to keep width and height proportional. Enter a higher value in either the Width or Height entry boxes. (The other entry box will update automatically if you have selected Constrain Proportions.)

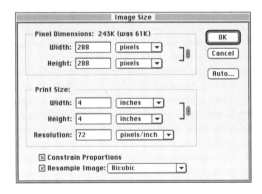

4 The overall dimensions of the image have now increased. The file size and total number of pixels have also increased, but the resolution remains the same.

Cropping an Image

Use the Crop tool to crop unwanted areas of an image and reduce the file size.

Press C on the keyboard to select the Crop tool, then press Return/Enter to show the Crop tool options palette.

1 Select the Crop tool from the Marquee group. You can double-click the tool to show the Crop tool options palette.

2 Position your cursor on the image, then click and drag to define the crop area. Don't worry if you don't get the crop exactly right first time.

Hold down Shift, then click and drag on a corner handle to resize the crop marquee in proportion.

3 • To reposition the crop marquee, place your cursor inside the marquee, then click and drag.

• To resize the crop marquee, place your cursor on one of the 8 handles around the marquee (the cursor changes to a bi-directional arrow), then click and drag.

The Crop tool snaps to the edge of the image. To prevent the snap effect, hold down Command/Ctrl as you create the crop marquee.

• To rotate the marquee, position your cursor just outside the marquee (the cursor changes shape to indicate rotation), then click and drag in a circular direction.

4 When you are satisfied with the position and size of the crop marquee, press Return/Enter to crop the picture. Alternatively, you can double-click inside the crop marquee. The areas outside the marquee are discarded. Press the Esc key if you do not want to accept the crop marquee.

Adding a Border

Borders are useful when you need additional space around the edges of your image.

Make sure that you select a background colour for your border, before you use the Canvas Size dialogue box.

1 Choose Image > Canvas Size. Use the measurement pop-up menus to choose a unit of measurement. Enter increased values for the width and/or height fields.

2 To specify where the border is added relative to the image, click one of the white placement squares. This sets the relative position of the image and the border. The grey square represents the position of the image, the white squares the position of the border.

3 OK the dialogue and the border is added, filled with the background colour.

Duotone Mode

You can only access Duotone mode when you have converted to greyscale.

Duotone is a very popular effect used to give added tonal depth to a greyscale image by printing with black and another colour.

When you start working with Photoshop, click on the Load button and try using one of the preset duotone settings that can be found in: Adobe Photoshop > Goodies > Duotone Presets > Duotones.

1 To create a duotone, choose Image > Mode > Duotone. The Duotone dialogue box appears. Choose from the pop-up whether you want to create a duotone (two inks), a tritone (three inks) or a quadtone (four inks).

2 To choose a second colour for the duotone, click the 'Ink 2' colour box (below the black ink box). This takes you into the Custom Colours dialogue box. Choose a colour. Click the Picker button if you want to use the Colour Picker. OK the dialogue box.

Make sure you save duotones in EPS format so that they colour separate correctly from page layout applications.

3 To specify the ink coverage for both colours, click on first the Ink 1 Curve box, then the Ink 2 box. In the Duotone Curve dialogue box. Drag the curve to the desired position, or enter values in the % entry boxes to adjust the ink coverage curve. OK both dialogue boxes to see the result.

Defining Colours

Defining colours is an essential aspect of using Photoshop and there is a range of techniques that can be used. The colour controls in the Toolbox indicate the current foreground and background colours.

Covers

Chapter Five

The Eyedropper and Colour Sampler Tools (I)

The Eyedropper Tool

The Eyedropper tool provides a quick and convenient way to pick up foreground and background colour from an area of the image you are working on, or from another inactive Photoshop image window.

1 To set the foreground colour, click on the Eyedropper tool.

2 Position your cursor, then click once on the image. (The foreground box in the Toolbox now represents the colour where you clicked.)

3 To set the background colour, hold down alt/Alt, then click on the image. The background box in the Toolbox now indicates the colour on which you clicked.

4 To set the Sample Size, use the Sample Size pop-up menu to choose a value. Point Sample reads the precise value of the pixel on which you click. 3 by 3 and 5 by 5 take average values of the pixels where you click.

 You can use the Eyedropper Options palette to specify the sample area of the image that the Eyedropper picks up. (Double-click the Eyedropper tool to show the Eyedropper Options palette if it is not already showing.)

The Colour Sampler Tool

Use the Colour Sampler tool, in conjunction with the Info palette, to set up to four sample points, which you can refer to as you make adjustments to colour values in the image. Each time you click in the image window with the Colour Sampler tool, you set a sample point. Each sample point you set creates an extra pane in the Info palette. To delete a sample point, drag it out of the image window using the Colour Sampler tool.

 To hide/ show the sample points, choose Hide/Show Sample Points from the Info palette pop-up.

The Colour Picker Palette

One of the most powerful and flexible ways of choosing foreground and background colours is using the Colour Picker palette. You can use a number of different colour models to create colour.

> 1 To create a Process colour using the Colour Picker, click once on either the foreground or background colour box. The Colour Picker dialogue box will appear.

Press the Tab key to move the highlight through the entry boxes in the dialogue box.

2 Enter values in the CMYK entry boxes. You will see a preview of the colour in the Current Colour swatch, which is above the Previous Colour swatch.

> 3 OK the dialogue box when you have mixed the colour you want. This now becomes the foreground or background colour, depending on which box you clicked in step 1.

...cont'd

You can also create colours using the Colour Slider and the Colour field. The next example looks at creating a colour using Hue, Saturation and Brightness values. You can apply the same techniques to Red, Green, Blue (RGB) and Lab colour models.

1 To create a colour using Hue, Saturation and Brightness (HSB) values, first click the Hue radio button.

2 Click on the Colour Slider bar, or drag the slider triangles on either side of the bar, to choose a hue or colour. This sets one of the three HSB values. The Hue entry box changes to a number that represents the hue you have chosen (0–360).

A warning triangle – the Gamut alarm – will appear next to the Current/ Previous colour boxes if you create a colour that cannot be printed using CMYK inks. Click the warning triangle to choose the nearest printable colour. The small box below the warning triangle indicates the nearest printable colour.

3 Next, click in the Colour Field to set the other two variables – Saturation and Brightness. Clicking to the left of the field reduces the saturation, clicking to the right increases the saturation of the selected hue. Clicking near the bottom decreases brightness, clicking near the top increases brightness for the selected hue.

4 If you click on the Saturation button, the Colour Slider now represents saturation (from 0–100) and the colour field allows you to choose Hue and Brightness values. When you click the Brightness radio button, the slider represents Brightness and the colour field represents Hue and Saturation.

Selecting Pantone Colours

You can access a range of colour-matching systems using the Colour Picker dialogue box. These include: Toyo Colour Finder 1050 System, Focoltone Colour System, Pantone Matching System, Trumatch Swatching System and DIC Colour Guide. Here, we'll select a Pantone colour.

1   To select a Pantone colour, click the foreground or background colour box. The Colour Picker dialogue box will appear. Click the Custom button.

2   Use the Book pop-up menu to select a Pantone matching system.

3   If you know the Pantone number of the colour you want, you can enter the number on the keyboard. Alternatively, click in the colour slider bar to the right of the Pantone colour boxes.

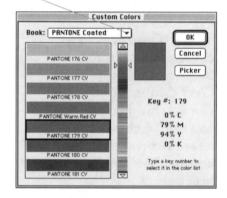

This moves you to a general range of colours. Then click on the scroll bars at the top and bottom of the sliders to find the specific Pantone colour you want.

4   Click on the colour you want to select, then click OK.

The Colour Palette

You can also use the Colour palette (Window > Show Colours) to mix new colours.

 If you click the active colour selection box, you will display the Colour Picker palette.

1 First identify which colour selection box is 'active'. There are two boxes, foreground and background. The active box is outlined in black.

2 Continue with step 3 if the correct box is active, or click the inactive box to make it the active box if necessary.

 During step 3, if you create a colour that is outside the CMYK colour gamut, the gamut alert warning triangle appears. You can click on the alert triangle to set the colour to the nearest CMYK equivalent. The nearest CMYK equivalent appears in a box next to the alert triangle.

3 Drag the colour slider triangles below the colour slider bars, or enter values in the entry boxes to the right of the palette. You can also click on a colour in the

Colour Bar running along the bottom of the Colour palette. The Colour Bar contains every colour in the CMYK spectrum as a default setting.

4 Use the pop-up triangle in the top right of the palette to change the colour model for sliders. Choose from Greyscale, RGB, HSB, CMYK, LAB sliders.

```
Grayscale Slider
✓ RGB Sliders
  HSB Sliders
  CMYK Sliders
  Lab Sliders

  Color Bar...
```

 Hold down Command (Mac) or Ctrl (Windows) and click the Colour bar to access the Colour Bar dialogue box.

5 You can also use the pop-up menu to change the Colour Bar setting. Choose Colour Bar..., then use the Style pop-up menu in the Colour Bar dialogue box to choose an option for the Colour Bar.

The Swatches Palette

You can use the Swatches palette (Window > Show Swatches) to set foreground and background colours, and you can also use it to create custom palettes which you can save and then reload into a different image.

See page 32 for details on loading and saving custom palette settings.

1 To select a foreground colour from the Swatches palette, click on a colour swatch.

2 To select a background colour, hold down alt/Alt and then click on a colour swatch.

You can customise the Swatches palette by adding and deleting colours in the palette.

Shift-clicking on an existing swatch replaces it with the current foreground colour. Pressing Shift and then alt/ Alt while clicking on a swatch inserts the current foreground colour to the left of the colour you click.

3 To add colour to the swatches, select a foreground colour. Position your cursor in an empty area of the Swatches palette. (The cursor changes to a paint bucket.) Then click to add the current foreground colour to the Swatches palette.

4 To delete a colour swatch, hold down Command (Mac) or Ctrl (Windows) and then click on a colour swatch.

The Painting Tools

The Paintbrush, Airbrush, Pencil, and Line tools apply the foreground colour to pixels in your image as you drag across them. Each painting tool creates a painting stroke with different characteristics. You can use the Brushes palette to determine the shape, size and type of the brush stroke for the Airbrush, Paintbrush, and Pencil tools.

All the painting and editing tools can be used within a selection or directly on an image.

Covers

Chapter Six

The Brushes Palette

The Brushes palette is central to using the painting and editing tools. Before you use any of these tools you need to check your brush size and shape. Choose Window > Show Brushes to show the Brushes palette.

1 To choose a hard-edged brush, click a brush in the first row of the default palette. To use a soft-edged brush, click one of the brushes in the second row. (The circle icons in the first two rows represent the actual size of the brush.) The third row contains brushes that are too large to be represented at their actual size. The number below them is the diameter of the brush in pixels.

You can use Brush Options from the pop-up menu to edit the settings for a selected brush.

2 To create a new brush, choose New Brush from the pop-up menu. Enter values for Diameter, Hardness, Spacing, Angle and Roundness in the New Brush dialogue box.

Diameter
Enter a value in pixels for the diameter of your brush from 1–999. Brush sizes too large to be represented at their actual size will display with the diameter indicated as a number.

Hardness

A setting of 100% gives a hard-edged brush. Settings below 100% produce soft-edged brushes. The lower you take this setting, the more diffuse the resultant stroke when you paint with the brush. Even with a setting of 100%, the edge of the brush-stroke is anti-aliased.

Spacing

Spacing is measured as a percentage of brush size. 25% is the default setting for all brushes. Higher settings begin to create non-continuous strokes.

Angle and Roundness

Use these controls together to create a stroke which thickens and thins like a calligraphic pen. You can enter values in the entry boxes, or drag the arrow indicator to change the angle, and drag the diameter dots to change the diameter.

3 OK the dialogue box. The new brush is added to the palette.

The keyline around it indicates that it is selected. (See page 32 for details on saving customised palettes for future use.)

To delete a brush, click on it to select it, then choose Delete brush in the pop-up menu.

New Brush...
Delete Brush

Brush Options...

Define Brush

Reset Brushes
Load Brushes...
Replace Brushes...
Save Brushes...

Painting Tool Techniques and Settings

Each painting tool has its own Options palette. There is a range of Options palette settings and techniques common to many of the painting and editing tools. Use the options covered here in conjunction with the specific controls for each of the tools on the following pages.

With a tool selected, press Return/Enter to show its Options palette.

Opacity, Pressure and Exposure

Opacity (Paintbrush, Line, Pencil, Eraser, Rubber Stamp), Pressure (Airbrush, Smudge, Focus tools) and Exposure (Toning tools) have a similar effect and determine the intensity of the tool you are working with. For example, opacity controls how completely pixels are covered by the foreground colour when you drag across them.

Make sure the Opacity/Pressure slider is at 100% if you want to completely cover the pixels you drag across. (Soft-edged brushes only partially cover pixels around the edge of the painting stroke to create the soft edge effect.) Reducing the Opacity/Pressure setting gives less complete results in the area you drag across, creating a semi-transparent, partially-covered effect.

Number keys on the keyboard can be used to set Opacity in increments of 10. (0 = 100%, 1 = 10%, 2 = 20% etc.) You can type two numbers in quick succession to specify other percentages.

Fade

Use the Fade setting to create the effect of paint on the painting tool running out as you drag across the image. The rate of Fade controls the number of pixels that are coloured before the paint fades to nothing. The higher the Fade setting, the further the paint goes before it fades out completely.

1 To set a fade rate for the Paintbrush, Airbrush or Pencil, double-click the tool to show the tool's Options palette.

2 Enter a fade value and use the Transparency/Background pop-up to specify what you want to fade to.

☒ Fade: 20	steps to	Transparent	▼
		• Transparent	
Stylus Pressure: ☐ Size		Background	

...cont'd

Undoing

To undo the last stroke you painted, choose Edit > Undo. This only works for the very last action you performed. In instances where you need to undo several steps, you can use the History palette. Use File > Revert to revert to the version of the file when you last saved it.

Cursor Types

Press Caps Lock to change painting and editing tool cursors to precise crosshairs. This is a very useful technique for making fine adjustments.

Whilst you are working with a painting tool, hold down alt/Alt to temporarily access the Eyedropper tool. This is useful for selecting a new foreground colour with which to paint.

2   Choose File > Preferences > Display and Cursors to change the way your painting tool cursors appear on-screen. 'Precise' has the same effect as pressing Caps Lock. 'Brush Size' is useful because you see the actual brush size represented on screen. (Changing the Painting Cursors preference to Precise reverses the effect of Caps Lock.)

Painting Tool Options Palettes

You can use the pop-up menu in each of the painting tool Options palettes to reset the default setting for the tool, or you can reset defaults for all tools.

The Paintbrush Tool (B)

The Paintbrush in Photoshop is like a normal paintbrush. You drag it across the pixels in your image and it colours those pixels with the foreground colour.

You can use a Fade setting to make the paint run out, just as with a normal paintbrush. You can also change the opacity setting to achieve a translucent, partial coverage of the pixels you drag across.

Remember to choose an appropriate brush size and shape before you begin painting.

| To paint with the Paintbrush, Line, Pencil or Airbrush, first double-click the tool to show the Options palette for that tool if it is not already showing.

2 Choose the settings you want, then position your cursor on the image, click and drag.

To constrain your painting strokes to straight lines, click with the painting tool to position the start of the stroke, move your cursor, (do not click and drag), then hold down Shift and click to end the stroke.

Wet Edges (Paintbrush & Eraser)
When you paint with wet edges selected you get a stroke that is darker around the edges and translucent inside the stroke, imitating the uneven build-up of paint in a watercolour.

Standard   Wet Edges

Fade = 60

The Airbrush Tool (J)

Use the Airbrush tool to imitate the effect of spraying paint with an airbrush. The airbrush paints with the foreground colour.

Use the Brushes palette to specify an Airbrush size and shape. Use a soft-edged brush to create the most realistic airbrush effect.

I   To paint with the Airbrush tool, double-click the Airbrush tool to display the Airbrush Options palette if it is not already showing. Use the palette to specify the settings for: Blending Mode, Pressure and Fade.

For a description of Blending modes see pages 82–83.

2   Click and drag across the image to apply the foreground colour. The more you spray over an area, the greater the build-up of colour. The speed at which you drag the airbrush also affects the intensity of the paint.

To change the Pressure setting using the keyboard, type a number on the keyboard. For example, type a 7 to specify a Pressure setting of 70%.

The Pencil and Line Tools (N)

The Pencil Tool

You can use the Pencil tool to draw freeform lines. The lines you draw with the Pencil tool are always hard-edged – in other words, the edges of your lines are not anti-aliased. The Pencil tool paints or draws with the foreground colour.

1 To draw a line, double-click the Pencil tool to show the Pencil Tool Options palette if it is not already showing. Use the Pencil Options palette to specify: Blending Mode, Opacity, Fade and Auto Erase options.

Use the Brushes palette to specify the size of your pencil.

2 Click and drag to create a freeform pencil stroke. Click, hold down Shift, then drag to constrain the pencil stroke vertically or horizontally. Click, move the cursor to a new position (do not click and drag), hold down Shift, then click again to create a straight pencil stroke between the two points.

Auto Erase

Select this option to use the Pencil tool as an eraser.

...cont'd

The Line Tool

Use the Line tool to create straight lines. Lines are filled with the foreground colour. Lines are always hard-edged.

 You cannot specify a brush size for the Line tool; use the Line Width setting in the Line Tool Options palette instead.

1 To draw a straight line, double-click the Line tool to show the Line Tool Options palette. Use the palette to specify Mode, Opacity and Line Width as desired.

2 Click and drag on the image to create a line. You can hold down Shift as you click and drag to constrain the line to 45-degree increments.

 You must specify arrowhead settings before you create a line.

3 To add arrowheads to the beginning or end of a line, click the Start/End options as appropriate. Click the Shape button to define the shape of the arrowhead.

4 Enter Width, Length and Concavity settings. OK the dialogue box, then click and drag to create the line.

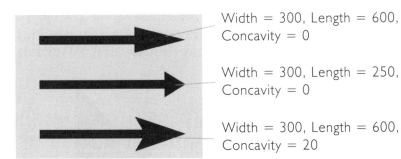

Width = 300, Length = 600, Concavity = 0

Width = 300, Length = 250, Concavity = 0

Width = 300, Length = 600, Concavity = 20

The Gradient Tool (G)

You can use the Gradient tools to create transitions from one colour to another. You can also create multi-coloured gradients. There are tools for Linear, Radial, Angle, Reflected and Diamond gradients. You can apply a gradient fill to a selection, or to an entire active layer.

1 To create a gradient fill, choose one of the Gradient tools and double-click the tool to show the Gradient Tool Options palette if it is not already showing.

2 Select a Blending mode and set Opacity. Use the gradient pop-up to choose from one of the preset gradients.

Hold down Shift as you click and drag to constrain a linear gradient to 45-degree increments.

3 Position your cursor where you want the gradient to start, then click and drag. The angle and distance you drag the cursor defines the angle and distance of a linear gradient, or the radius of a radial gradient. (Click and drag from the centre out to create Radial, Angle, Reflected and Diamond gradient fills.)

4 For basic gradient fills leave the Transparency and Dither options selected.

For a linear gradient, the start and end colours fill any part of the selection that you do not drag the cursor across. For radial gradients, the end colour fills the remaining area.

Linear

Radial

Angle

Reflected

Diamond

The Paint Bucket Tool (K)

You can use the Paint Bucket tool to colour pixels with the foreground colour, based on a tolerance setting. It works in a similar way to the Magic Wand tool, but in this case, filling adjoining pixels that fall within the tolerance setting. You can use the Paint Bucket tool within a selection or on the entire image.

1 To fill an area with the foreground colour, double-click the Paint Bucket tool to show the Paint Bucket Options palette if it is not already showing. Enter a value from 0–255 in the Tolerance box. The higher you set the value, the greater the range of pixels the Paint Bucket will fill.

 The Anti-aliased option creates a slightly soft edge on the areas that the Paint Bucket fills.

2 Set Opacity, Blending mode, Anti-aliased and Sample Merged options. Position your cursor then click on the image.

3 You can use the Paint Bucket to fill with a pattern previously saved into the pattern buffer. Use the Contents pop-up to specify whether the Paint Bucket fills with the foreground colour or a pattern.

 You cannot use the Paint Bucket on images in Bitmap mode.

Blending Modes

The blending modes allow you to make changes to an image using the painting and editing tools in a more selective and subtle way than simply painting with the foreground colour. The colour you paint with (the blend colour) combines with the colour of the pixels you drag across (the base colour) to produce a different colour depending on the blending mode you select.

Choose blending modes from the pop-up menu in the Painting Tool Options palettes. The various paint modes in combination with opacity/pressure settings have a selective control on which pixels are affected when you use the painting and editing tools. The result is more of a blending of the paint colour and the colour of the base pixels than simply one colour replacing another.

Dissolve

Produces a grainy, chalk-like effect. Not all pixels are coloured as you drag across the image, leaving gaps and holes in the stroke. Use Opacity to control the effect.

Behind

Only available when you are working on a layer with a transparent background. Use Behind to paint behind the existing pixels on a layer. Paint appears in the transparent areas, but does not affect the existing pixels.

Multiply

Combines the colour you are painting with the colour of the pixels you drag across, to produce a colour that is darker than the original colours.

Screen

Produces the opposite effect to Multiply. It multiplies the opposite of the original colour by the painting colour and has the effect of lightening the pixels.

Blending modes are also available in the Layers palette and in the Fill Path, Fill, Stroke and Fade dialogue boxes.

Overlay

This increases the contrast and saturation, combining foreground colour with the pixels you drag across.

Soft Light

Creates a soft lighting effect. Lightens colours if the painting colour is lighter than 50% grey, darkens colours if the painting colour is darker than 50% grey.

...cont'd

 Use the Opacity/ Pressure setting to control the intensity of the effect.

 Be prepared to experiment with blending modes to fully understand their results and to get the best out of them.

Hard Light
Multiplies or screens pixels, depending on the paint colour, and tends to increase contrast.

Darken
Applies the paint colour to pixels that are lighter than the paint colour – doesn't change pixels darker than the paint colour.

Lighten
Replaces pixels darker than the paint colour, but does not change pixels lighter than the paint colour.

Difference
It looks at the brightness of pixels and the paint colour, then subtracts paint brightness from pixel brightness. Depending on the result, it inverts the pixels.

Exclusion
The result is similar to Difference, but with lower contrast.

Hue
In colour images, applies the hue (colour) of the paint, without affecting the saturation or luminosity of the base pixels.

Saturation
Changes the saturation of pixels based on the saturation of the blend colour, but does not affect hue or luminosity.

Luminosity
Changes the relative lightness or darkness of the pixels without affecting their hue or saturation.

Colour
Applies the hue and saturation of the blend colour, but does not affect the luminosity of the base pixels.

Colour Dodge
Lightens the base colour – more pronounced when the paint colour is light.

Colour Burn
Darkens the base colour – more pronounced when paint colour is dark.

Defining a Brush

You can create your own custom brush strokes from selections.

1 To create a brushstroke, make a selection, then choose Define Brush from the pop-up menu in the Brushes palette. The new brush is added to the Brushes palette.

2 Double-click the brush if you want to change the spacing and anti-aliased options. Anti-aliased is not available for very large brush sizes.

3 You can then use a painting tool to paint with the new brush. In this example a fade of 30 has been set.

The Editing Tools

The editing tools – Blur and Sharpen, Smudge, Rubber and Pattern Stamp, Dodge, Burn, Sponge and Eraser – allow you to edit or change pixels in a variety of ways.

The editing tools can be used within a selection or anywhere on an image. Use the Brushes palette to specify a brush size for the editing tool. Many of the techniques and keyboard shortcuts covered for the painting tools apply to the editing tools as well.

Covers

Chapter Seven

The Blur, Sharpen and Smudge Tools (R)

The Blur Tool

The Blur and Sharpen tools are the two 'Focus' tools. The Blur tool works by reducing contrast between pixels and can be useful for disguising unwanted, jagged edges and softening edges between shapes.

Remember to set an appropriate brush size before you start working with the Blur/Sharpen tool.

To blur areas of your image, select the Blur tool. If the Blur Options palette is not showing, you can double-click the Blur tool to show it.

2 Set the Blend (Effect) mode, Pressure and Use All Layers options, position your cursor on the image, then click and drag to blur the pixels. Release the mouse then drag across the pixels again to intensify the effect.

You cannot use the Blur/ Sharpen tool on an image in bitmap or indexed colour mode.

The Sharpen Tool

The Sharpen tool works by increasing the contrast between pixels.

To sharpen areas of an image, select the Sharpen tool. Double-click the Sharpen tool to show the Sharpen Options palette.

Each Focus tool retains its own settings when you switch to the other tool.

2 Position your cursor, then click and drag to sharpen the pixels. Click and drag across the same area of the image again, to intensify the sharpening effect. You will produce a coarse, grainy effect if you overuse the Sharpen tool. Use a low pressure setting and build up the effect gradually.

...cont'd

The Smudge Tool

You can use the Smudge tool to create an effect similar to dragging your finger through wet paint. The Smudge tool picks up colour from where you start to drag and smears it into adjacent colours.

1 Double-click the Smudge tool to show the Smudge Tool Options palette if it is not already showing. Set the pressure, position your cursor on the image, then start to drag across your image to smudge the colours. The higher the pressure setting, the more pronounced the effect.

Hold down alt/Alt to temporarily turn Finger Painting on or off, depending on whether the option is selected in the Options palette.

2 Select the Finger Painting option if you want to begin the smudge with the current foreground colour.

3 Select the Use All Layers option if you want to smudge colours from other layers in the image onto the layer you are working on. Leave this option deselected if you want the smudge to pick up colour from pixels on the active or target layer only.

Use All Layers

Select this option when you want Photoshop to take into account, or 'sample', pixels from layers other than the target layer. In other words, it samples from layers as if they were merged.

The Rubber and Pattern Stamp Tools (S)

You can use the Rubber Stamp tool to retouch your image by cloning or duplicating areas of your image. This is very useful when you want to remove blemishes and scratches from images. Use the Pattern Stamp tool to paint with a predefined pattern.

The Rubber Stamp Tool

1   To clone an area of your image, double-click the Rubber Stamp tool to show the Rubber Stamp Options palette if it is not already showing. Remember to set an appropriate brush size.

2   Make sure that the Aligned option is selected. Hold down alt/Alt and click on the part of the image you want to clone.

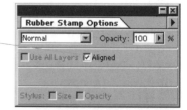

3   Release alt/Alt. Move your cursor to a different part of your image, then click and drag. The pixels in the image where you drag are replaced by pixels cloned from the spot where you first clicked. A crosshair at the point where you first clicked indicates the pixels that are being cloned – the source point.

Clone – Aligned

With the Aligned option selected, the distance from the source point (represented by the crosshair) to the Rubber Stamp cursor remains fixed. This means that you can release the mouse, move the cursor, then continue to use the Rubber Stamp tool. The relative position of the source point and the Rubber Stamp cursor remain constant, but you will now be cloning pixels from a different part of the image.

...cont'd

Clone – Non-aligned

With the Aligned option off, the source point – where you first click – remains the same. If you stop dragging with the Rubber Stamp cursor, move to a different part of the image, then start dragging again, the pixels you clone continue to come from the original source point.

The Pattern Stamp Tool

The Pattern Stamp tool works in a similar way to the Rubber Stamp tool, but it paints with a predefined area of pixels – the pattern – rather than from a variable source point in the image.

To define a pattern, select an area to use as a pattern (using the rectangular marquee tool: ⬚ – see page 94), then choose Edit > Define Pattern.

2 Choose the Pattern Stamp Tool. Check your brush size, position your cursor on the image, then click and drag to paint with the pattern.

Pattern – Aligned

With the Aligned option selected, even if you stop dragging and then restart, the pattern aligns seamlessly.

Pattern – Non-aligned

This option paints with the predefined pattern, but does not align seamlessly if you stop dragging and then restart dragging.

Use All Layers

Select this option if you want to sample pixels from all layers when you define a source point. Leave this option deselected to sample pixels from the target layer only.

The Dodge, Burn and Sponge Tools (O)

The Dodge, Burn, Saturate/Desaturate group of tools are collectively called the 'Toning' tools. The Dodge and Burn tools are based on the traditional photographic technique of decreasing the amount of exposure given to a specific area on a print to lighten it (dodging), or increasing the exposure to darken areas (burning-in).

The Dodge Tool
Use the Dodge tool to lighten pixels in your image.

You cannot use the Dodge, Burn or Saturate/Desaturate tools on an image in Bitmap or Indexed Colour mode.

1 To lighten areas of an image, select the Dodge tool. Remember to choose an appropriate brush size. A soft-edged brush usually creates the smoothest result. If the Toning Tools Options palette is not showing, you can double-click the Dodge tool to show it.

2 Set the Midtone/Shadow/Highlight pop-up to limit changes to the middle range of greys, the dark or light areas of the image respectively, and also set Exposure to control the intensity of the tool.

It's a good idea to use a low exposure setting when you lighten areas of an image and build up the effect gradually.

3 Position your cursor on the image, then click and drag to lighten the pixels. Release the mouse then drag across the pixels again to intensify the effect.

The Burn Tool

Use the Burn tool to darken pixels in your image.

1 To darken areas of an image, select the Burn tool. Remember to choose an appropriate brush size. A soft-edged brush usually creates the smoothest result. If the Burn Options palette is not showing, you can double-click the Burn tool to show it.

2 Set the Midtone/Shadow/Highlight pop-up to limit changes to the middle range of greys, the dark or light areas of the image respectively, and also set Exposure.

3 Position your cursor on the image, then click and drag to lighten the pixels. Release the mouse then drag across the pixels again to intensify the effect.

In Greyscale Mode, the Sponge tool has the effect of increasing or decreasing contrast.

The Sponge Tool

You can use the Sponge tool when you want to subtly increase or decrease colour saturation in areas of your image.

1 To saturate/desaturate areas of an image, select the Sponge tool. Remember to select an appropriate brush size. If the Sponge Options palette is not showing, you can double-click the Sponge tool.

Each Toning tool retains its own settings when you switch to the other tools in the same group.

2 Set options for Saturate/ Desaturate and Pressure.

3 Position your cursor on the image, then click and drag to alter the saturation.

The Eraser Tool (E)

Use the Eraser tool to erase portions of your image. The Eraser rubs out to the background colour when you are working on the Background layer. It erases to transparency when you are working on any other layer, provided that the Preserve Transparency option is off.

Use the Brushes palette to specify the Eraser size when using the tool in Paintbrush, Pencil and Airbrush mode.

1 To erase areas of your image, double-click the Eraser tool to show the Eraser Options palette. Use the palette to specify Type, Opacity, Fade, Wet Edges and Erase to History options.

2 Click and drag on your image to erase to the background colour or transparency, depending on the layer on which you are working.

Hold down alt/Alt with the Eraser tool selected to access the Erase to History option temporarily. Click and drag across modified areas of the image to restore them to the specified state in the History palette.

Opacity

Use the opacity setting to create the effect of partially erasing pixels.

Mode

Use the Erasing Mode pop-up to choose an erase mode. The default is Paintbrush.

Erase to History

Use the Erase to History option to return pixels to their status at a particular state in the History palette. Click in the History Brush column in the History palette to set the state to which the Erase to History option returns pixels.

Making Selections

One of the most important techniques when using Photoshop is making selections. When you make a selection, you are selecting an area of the image to which you want to make changes, and isolating the remainder of the image so that it is not affected by changes. A selection is indicated on-screen by a selection marquee – sometimes referred to as the 'marching ants' border.

Covers

Chapter Eight

The Marquee Selection Tool (M)

The Marquee selection tools allow you to drag with the mouse to make selections. You can make rectangular or elliptical selections by choosing the appropriate tool.

 If you are working on an image with more than one layer, make sure you select the appropriate target layer before you make a selection.

1 To make a rectangular or oval selection, choose the Rectangular or Elliptical Marquee tool.

 Hold down Shift, then click and drag with the Rectangular or Elliptical Marquee tool to create a square or circular selection. Hold down alt/Alt to create a selection from the centre out.

2 Position your cursor on the image, then click and drag to define the area you want to select. When you release the cursor you will see a dotted rectangular or oval marquee defining the area of the selection.

3 You can reposition the selection marquee if you need to. Make sure the Marquee tool is still selected, position your cursor inside the selection marquee (the cursor changes shape), then click and drag. You can move selection marquees with any of the Selection tools.

 As you are dragging to create a selection, you can hold down the spacebar to reposition the marquee.

4 With the Marquee tool selected, you can deselect a selection by clicking inside or outside the selection marquee. Alternatively, you can choose Select > Deselect.

Marquee Options

You can use the Marquee Options palette to make changes to the way in which the Marquee tools work.

You can only have one selection active at a time, although a selection can consist of several non-contiguous areas.

1. Double-click the Marquee tool. The Marquee Options palette will appear if it is not already showing. Alternatively, select a Marquee tool, then choose Window > Show Options.

2. Use the Style pop-up to create settings for making proportional selections, or selections of a fixed size.

The Anti-aliased option is available in the Elliptical Marquee, Lasso and Magic Wand Options palettes.

3. The Anti-aliased option is an important control when using bitmap applications such as Photoshop. Select anti-aliased to create a slightly blurred, soft edge around the selection and the pixels that surround the selection. Using Anti-aliased helps avoid creating unwanted jagged edges.

Choose Select > Reselect to reselect your most recent selection. You can use the Reselect command even if you have performed operations and commands on the image since you deselected.

4. Use the Feather entry field to create a soft, feathered edge. (See pages 102–103 in this chapter.)

Moving Selections

You can use the Selection tools to reposition a selection border, but you must use the Move tool if you want to move pixels from one location to another.

Make a selection. Select the Move tool and then position your cursor inside the Marquee selection border. Click and drag to move the selection. Alternatively, with the Marquee, Lasso or Magic Wand tool still selected, hold down Command/Ctrl. The cursor changes temporarily to the Move tool cursor. Click and drag to move the selected pixels.

When you move pixels on the Background layer, the area from which the pixels are moved is filled with the current background colour.

As long as the selection border remains selected, you can continue to move the pixels. Whilst the selection is active, the pixels in the selection 'float' above the underlying pixels, without replacing them.

2 To 'defloat' the pixels so that they replace the underlying pixels, choose Select > Deselect if you have the Move tool selected. If you used Command/Ctrl with a Marquee or Lasso tool selected, click outside the selection marquee. If you used Command/Ctrl with the Magic Wand tool selected, choose Select > Deselect. As soon as you deselect, the pixels on the Background layer that were underneath the floating selection – the underlying pixels – are now completely replaced by the pixels in the floating selection.

To move the selection in increments of one pixel with the Move tool selected, press the up, down, left or right arrow keys. Hold down Shift and press the arrow keys to move the selection in increments of five pixels.

3 Notice that the area that the pixels in the selection were moved from is filled with the currently selected background colour. (In a bitmap image, you cannot have an area where there are no pixels.)

4 To move a selection and make a copy of it at the same time, hold down alt/Alt before you drag with the Move tool. Alternatively, with a selection tool selected, hold down Command/Ctrl+alt/Alt,

then click and drag. The cursor turns into a double-headed arrow, indicating that you are copying the selection.

5 You can turn a 'floating' selection into a layer by choosing Layer > New > Layer Via Cut. (See Chapter 9 – Layers for further information.)

The Lasso Tools (L)

You can use the Lasso tool to make freeform selections by clicking and dragging. It is a useful tool for selecting irregular areas and for quickly adding to or subtracting from selections made with the Magic Wand tool.

Hold down Shift, then click and drag around an area to add it to the selection. Hold down alt/Alt, then click and drag around an area to remove it from the selection.

1 Double-click the Lasso tool to show the Lasso Options palette if it is not already showing. Set Feather and Anti-aliased options.

2 Position your cursor on the image. The cursor changes to the Lasso cursor. Click and drag around the part of the image you want to select. Make sure your cursor comes back to the start point. If you release before reaching the start point, Photoshop completes the selection with a straight line. A dotted marquee defines the selected area.

Polygon Lasso

Use the Polygon Lasso tool to create a freeform selection with straight line segments.

If you have a feather amount set in the Lasso Options palette, you will not end up with sharp corners on the selection.

1 Select the Polygon Lasso tool. Position your cursor on the image, then click; move the cursor, then click… and so on, until you have defined the area you want to select.

2 Click back at the start point to complete the selection. A small circle appears at the bottom right of the cursor to indicate the start. Alternatively, you can double-click to close the selection marquee.

The Magnetic Lasso

The Magnetic Lasso Tool is most useful when you want to select an object or an area of the image which contrasts strongly with the area surrounding it.

1 Press and hold on the Lasso tool, to select the Magnetic Lasso tool from the tool group. Click on the edge of the object you want to select to place the first fastening point.

2 Either, move the cursor along the edge of the object, or click and drag along the edge to draw a freehand segment. As you move along the edge of the object, the 'active' segment of the selection border snaps to the most clearly defined edge in the image (in the close proximity of the cursor). Fastening points are added automatically, at intervals, as you drag.

A fastening point anchors the Selection Border in place as you create the selection. Fastening Points disappear when you close the selection border. The Magnetic Lasso adds fastening points at intervals to the selection border to anchor the segments.

3 Click on the edge of the shape if you need to add a fastening point manually. Continue moving the cursor, or dragging and clicking, to continue making the selection border.

4 To close the selection border, position your cursor on the start point, (a small circle at the cursor indicates that you are on the start point) then click. Alternatively, double-click, or press the Enter/Return key. Photoshop will create a segment from the point you have reached to the start point of the selection border. To close the selection border with a straight line segment, hold down alt/ALT and double-click.

...cont'd

Double-click the Magnetic Lasso tool to show the Magnetic Lasso Options palette if it is not already showing. (Or use Window > Show Options.)

Magnetic Lasso Options

As with all the tools you use in Photoshop, after you have clicked on the tool to select it, but before you start to use it, check the setting for the tool in the appropriate tool options palette.

Lasso Width

Enter a value between 1–40 to specify a detection width. The Magnetic Lasso tool detects edges only within the specified distance from the pointer.

Frequency

this setting determines the rate at which Fastening points are set. Enter a value between 0–100. The higher the value you set, the more frequently fastening points are placed.

Edge Contrast

Enter a value between 1–100%. This value determines how sensitive the Magnetic Lasso tool is to edges in the image. Higher values select edges that contrast strongly with their background. Lower values select edges that have smaller amounts of contrast.

If the object you are trying to select has high contrast (ie, well defined edges) use higher Lasso Width and Edge Contrast settings. For objects with less well defined edges, use lower Lasso Width and Edge Contrast settings.

The Magic Wand Tool (W)

The Magic Wand tool is useful for selecting continuous areas of colour in an image, based on a tolerance setting. A low tolerance setting will make a very limited selection of colour. A high setting will select a wider range of pixels. The tool is good for selecting consistently coloured areas, without having to trace the outline with the Lasso tool.

To add to a selection using the Magic Wand tool, hold down Shift, then click on an unselected part of the image.

1 Before you create a selection using the Magic Wand tool, check the tolerance setting. Double-click the Magic Wand tool to display the Magic Wand Options palette, or choose

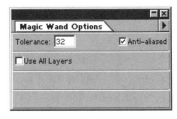

Window > Show Options to show the Tool Options palette, then select the Magic Wand tool. Enter a tolerance value from 0–255. If you set the maximum tolerance value of 255, you will select every pixel in the image.

Typically, you will fine-tune Magic Wand selections using a combination of the other selection tools, together with the Grow and Similar commands.

2 Click on the image where you want to select pixels of similar colour value. All adjacent pixels that are within the tolerance range are selected. When you begin working

with the Magic Wand tool, start off using the default setting of 32 and then adjust this as necessary to make the selection you require.

You cannot use the Magic Wand tool in Bitmap mode.

3 To deselect a selection marquee when the Magic Wand tool is selected, click inside the selection marquee. If you click outside the selection marquee, you will create another selection based around the pixel where you clicked.

Feathering Selections

You can define a feathered edge when you make selections using the Lasso tools and the Marquee tools.

You can use the Feather option to control the degree to which the edge of a selection is softened or faded. Feathering a selection creates a transition boundary between the selection and the surrounding pixels, which can cause a loss of detail.

1 Double-click one of the Lasso or the Marquee selection tools. The Options palette for the tool appears if it was not already showing.

Check the Options palette before you make a selection to make sure that there isn't a feather amount set if you don't want one.

2 In the Options palette, set a feather value, e.g. 10. You can set a value from 1 to 250 pixels. The amount you set depends on the effect you want to achieve.

3 Create a selection using either the Marquee or Lasso tool. When you move the selection you will see the feathered edge around the selection and also where you move the selection from.

When you set a feather amount, the selection you make may appear more 'rounded' than you expect. This is caused by the feather value.

4 Alternatively, you can make a selection and then choose Select > Feather. Enter a value for the Feather radius.

Creating a Vignette

You can use the feathering option to create a vignette effect – a soft, fading edge to an image.

1 Before you begin, make sure your background colour is set to white (see Chapter Five – Defining Colours). Then set a feather value in the Options palette for the selection tool you are using.

2 Next, create a selection, which can be a regular or irregular shape.

3 Choose Select > Inverse. This reverses the selection – selecting all the pixels that were previously not selected.

Feathering, unlike anti-aliasing, blurs the inside and outside of a selection boundary.

4 Press Delete (Mac) or Backspace (Windows) to delete the area surrounding your selection, leaving a feathered edge.

Modifying Selections

There are many instances when you need to add to or subtract from a selection. You can use any combination of selection tools to make the selection you want. For example, you might start by making a selection with the Magic Wand tool, then add to the selection using the Lasso tool.

For complex selections, it can be quite useful to hide the dotted selection border temporarily, in order to see the selected pixels more clearly. Choose View > Hide Edges to hide the selection border. The selection remains active; you have simply hidden the border. Choose View > Show Edges to redisplay the selection border.

1 To add to an existing selection, hold down the Shift key, then click and drag to create another selection marquee that intersects the existing selection marquee.

2 You can use the same technique to create non-adjoining selections. Although the selections may be in different parts of the image, they count and act as one selection. So, for example, if you apply a filter, the effect will be apparent in all the selection marquees.

3 Hold down Shift and use the Lasso tool to quickly loop around small areas that the Magic Wand tool typically misses out from its selection.

4 To subtract from a selection, hold down alt/Alt, then click and drag with a selection tool to intersect the existing selection marquee. The area defined by the intersecting marquee will be removed from the original selection.

The Grow and Similar Commands

The Grow and Similar commands are very useful when used in conjunction with the Magic Wand tool to add to a selection. Both work according to the tolerance setting set in the Magic Wand Options palette.

The Grow command selects contiguous or adjoining areas of colour based on the tolerance setting in the Magic Wand Options palette.

1 Make a selection. Check that the Tolerance setting in the Magic Wand Options palette is appropriate.

2 Choose Select > Grow. Pixels which fall within the Tolerance setting and are adjacent to pixels already in the selection are added to the selection.

The Similar command selects non-adjacent pixels that fall within the same tolerance setting as set in the Magic Wand Options palette.

1 Make a selection using any of the selection tools. Check that the Tolerance setting in the Magic Wand Options palette is appropriate.

2 Choose Select > Similar. Pixels throughout the image that fall within the Tolerance setting are selected.

Pasting Into Selections

Pasting into selections is a useful technique for compositing images.

When you paste into a selection, the selection from the clipboard will be rendered at the resolution of the destination document. This means that the selection from the source document will change size if the resolution of the two documents is different.

Make sure the layer mask is selected, then paint with black to add to the mask, or paint with white to subtract from the mask. (See pages 156–157, 'Layer Masks'.)

1 Create a selection in the destination window.

2 Open the source document, then make the selection you want to paste into the destination document. Choose Edit > Copy to copy the selection to the clipboard.

3 Click in the destination image window. The selection should still be active. Choose Edit > Paste Into to paste the clipboard selection into the selected area.

4 Use the Move tool to reposition the pasted selection relative to the original selection.

5 The Paste Into command has created a layer mask. The layer is active, indicated by the paintbrush icon in the Layers palette, which means that you can edit the layer. To edit the mask, click the mask icon in the Layers palette. A small circle replaces the paintbrush, indicating that the layer mask is selected.

The Defringe Command

You can drag a selection from one window to another image window. This is useful when creating a composite image. Defringe is useful when you use this technique, as it helps to blend the selection into its new environment.

1 To drag a selection from one image window to another, first make a selection in the source window. Select the Move tool, position the Move cursor inside the selection, then click and drag into the destination window.

2 When you release the mouse button, the selection appears in the destination window on a new layer. The destination window becomes the active window, and the new layer is the active layer. Check to see if there are unwanted pixels causing a halo effect around the edge of the selection.

A width setting of 1 or 2 pixels is usually sufficient to defringe a pasted or moved selection.

3 To defringe the moved selection, make sure the newly created layer is active, and make sure Preserve Transparency is deselected. Choose Layer > Matting > Defringe. Enter a value for the width, then OK the dialogue box. The selection should now blend in better.

Filling a Selection

You can use the Fill dialogue box to fill an entire layer or a selection.

1 To fill a selection, first define either a foreground or background colour that you want to fill with, then make a selection. Choose Edit > Fill. Use the Contents pop-up to choose the fill type. You can also set Opacity for the fill and a Blending Mode. OK the dialogue box.

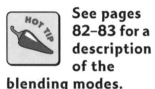

See pages 82–83 for a description of the blending modes.

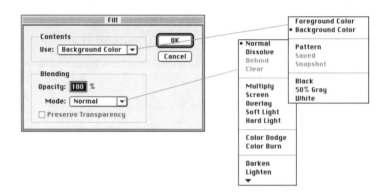

2 To fill a selection with a pattern, first define the pattern by making a selection, then choosing Edit > Define Pattern.

3 Choose Edit > Fill. Choose Pattern from the Contents pop-up. OK the dialogue box to fill the selection with the pattern.

Copying and Pasting Selections

You can use the clipboard to copy and past selections within the same image and into other images.

A useful technique for selecting a simple image, like the runner on this page, is the Inverse selection command. Use the Magic Wand tool to select the background, then choose Select > Inverse to reverse the selection. The areas that represent the runner are now selected.

1 To copy a selection, first make a selection using any of the selection tools. Choose Edit > Copy.

2 To paste the selection into the same image, choose Edit > Paste. The selection is pasted into the image on its own layer. (For information on working with layers, see Chapter Nine, 'Layers'.)

3 To paste the selection into another image, click on the other image window if it is already open, or use File > Open to open another image. Choose Edit > Paste to paste the selection from the clipboard onto a new layer in the active image.

4 You can also drag a selection from one image window into another. You need two images open – the source and the destination windows. Make a selection in the source window, select the Move tool, position your cursor within the selection, then click and drag into the destination window. The selection appears on its own layer.

Use the Defringe command (see page 107) to help a pasted or dragged selection blend into its new surroundings.

Transforming Selections

The ability to transform a selection's bounding box enables you to fine tune selections, distort selections and make selections that were previously difficult to achieve.

The Transform Selection bounding box transforms the selection border only. It does not transform the pixels within the selection.

Drag the point of origin to a new location to specify the point around which transformations take place.

1 To transform a selection, choose Select > Transform Selection. A bounding box with eight handles appears around the selection. A Point of Origin marker appears at the centre of the bounding box.

2 To scale a selection, click and drag a handle. The cursor becomes a bi-directional arrow (⤢). To scale a selection in proportion, hold down Shift then drag a handle.

3 To rotate a selection, position your cursor just outside the selection border. The cursor changes to a bi-directional, curved arrow (↻). Click and drag in a circular direction.

4 To distort the selection boundary, hold down Command/Ctrl then drag a corner handle.

5 To create a perspective effect on the selection border, hold down Command/Ctrl+alt/ Alt+Shift, then drag a corner handle.

6 To shear a selection border, hold down Command/Ctrl, then click and drag a centre top/bottom or centre left/right handle.

7 Press the Esc key to remove the transform bounding box without applying any of the changes. Press return/Enter, or double-click inside the bounding box to accept the transformation.

Layers

Layers introduce a considerable degree of flexibility into the way in which you can work in Photoshop. Layers allow you to keep various elements of your image separate so that you can make changes without deleting or changing the underlying pixels in the image.

Each additional layer you create increases the file size of the image. When you have finished editing your image, you can selectively merge layers into each other. You will need to do this to use your image in QuarkXPress or Adobe PageMaker. You should note that you can only save images with layers in Photoshop format.

When you create or open an image for the first time, it consists of one default layer called Background.

Covers

Chapter Nine

Working with Layers

To access the Layers palette, choose Window > Show Layers.

New layers are automatically created when you use the Type tool to add text to an image, when you drag or copy a selection into an image, and also when you drag a layer from one document into another.

I To create a new layer, either click once on the New Layer icon at the bottom of the Layers palette, or use the pop-up menu in the Layers palette and choose New Layer.

2 Enter a name for the layer in the New Layer dialogue box. You can also choose Opacity and Blending Mode settings at this stage if you want to.

3 OK the dialogue box, or press Return/Enter. The new layer appears in the Layers palette above the previously highlighted layer. Notice also that the file size in the Document Sizes status bar area increases when you paint on the layer or add pixels to the layer.

To edit Layer Options for a Layer, double-click the layer name. The Layer Options dialogue box appears. Make changes as necessary, then OK the dialogue box.

4 To delete a layer, click on the layer to select it. Then choose Delete Layer from the pop-up menu in the Layers palette. Click Yes or No in the Delete Layer warning box. Alternatively, drag the Layer name onto the Wastebasket icon at the bottom of the Layers palette.

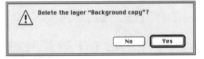

Selecting, Hiding and Showing Layers

You can only work on one layer at a time. This is often referred to as the 'target' or active layer.

You can nudge the contents of a selected layer in 1-pixel increments by pressing the arrow keys when the Move tool is selected.

1. Click on the layer name in the Layers palette to make it active. The layer name will highlight and the paintbrush icon will appear in the second column on the left of the palette.

2. To hide a layer, click on the eye icon in the leftmost column of the Layers palette. To show a layer, click in the leftmost column to bring back the eye icon.

Reordering Layers

It is often necessary to reorder the stacking position of layers, in order to control which layers appear in front of other layers.

You can move pixels in a layer beyond the edge of your picture. These non-visible pixels will be saved with the document. These non-visible pixels are lost when you flatten the image.

1. To change the layering order, click and drag the layer name you want to reposition. Notice the black horizontal bar that appears as you move the layer upwards or downwards. Release the mouse when the black bar appears in the position to which you want the layer moved.

Repositioning Layers

You can reposition the entire contents of a layer using the Move tool.

Click on the layer you want to move in the Layers palette. Select the Move tool, then position your cursor anywhere on the image. Click and drag to move the layer.

Merging and Flattening Layers

The Merge Visible Layers command in the pop-up menu merges only the currently visible layers.

Use the Merge commands to combine two or more layers into one layer. This is useful for keeping file size down and for consolidating elements on different layers into a single manageable layer or unit.

To merge all the visible layers in your document, first hide any layers you don't want to merge, make sure one of the layers you want to merge is active, then choose Merge Visible from the pop-up menu in the Layers palette, or choose Layer > Merge Visible.

When you use the Flatten Image command, any hidden layers will be discarded.

2 To merge a layer with the layer below it, first select the layer, then choose Merge Down from the pop-up menu, or choose Layer > Merge Down.

When you convert images between some modes you are prompted to flatten the file. Make sure you save a copy of the file first if you want to be able to go back and make further changes to the layers.

Flattening Images

When you flatten an image, you end up with a Background layer only. This reduces the file size. Flatten an image when you have finished creating and positioning the elements of your composite image, and are ready to save the file in a suitable format for placing in a page layout application.

To flatten an image, make sure that all the layers you want to keep are visible. Choose Flatten Image from the Layers palette pop-up menu, or choose Layers > Flatten Image.

Moving Layers Between Images

The layer you move into the destination image window is rendered at the resolution of the destination window. This may cause the elements on the moved layer to appear larger or smaller than in the original window. To avoid surprises, make sure that the source and destination images are at the same resolution.
Also, if the modes of the two images are different, the layer you move will be converted to match the mode of the destination window.

You can copy a complete layer from one Photoshop document to another, similar to the way you move a selection from one document to another.

1   First make sure you have two document windows open – a 'source' document and a 'destination' document. The source document contains the layer you want to copy. The destination document is the document into which you want to copy the layer.

2   Click in the source document window to make it active. Position your cursor on the layer in the Layers palette, then drag the layer you want to copy from the source document into the destination document window. You will see a bounding box indicating the layer you are copying.

Use the Defringe command (see page 107) to remove any fringe around pixels on a layer that you copy from one image to another.

3   Position the layer and then release the mouse. The layer is positioned above the previously active layer in the Layers palette of the destination document. The destination document is now the active image window.

Linking Layers

Linking layers is useful when you want to keep elements of an image on separate layers, but you need to move the layers maintaining the exact positional relationship of each.

The principle of linking layers works, even if the layers are not next to each other in the Layers palette.

1 To move the foreground object with its shadow (which is on a separate layer), show the Layers palette (Window > Show Layers) and make sure that one of the layers you want to link is active.

2 Click in the empty box to the right of the eye icon of the layer you want to link. A chain icon appears in the box, indicating that the layer is linked. When you make the linked layer active, the chain and paintbrush icons switch to indicate the layer you are working on.

3 Use the Move tool to reposition the elements on the linked layers as one.

4 You can link multiple layers using the same technique.

5 To unlink a layer, click the chain icon. The layer is now completely independent again.

Adjustment Layers

Using an adjustment layer is like positioning a lens above the pixels on the layers below it to change their appearance. If you don't like the result, you can edit the adjustment layer to achieve the result you want, or you can discard the adjustment layer. When you are satisfied with the result you can implement the adjustment layer as a permanent change.

An adjustment layer is created above the currently active layer. Its settings are applied to the layers below it and do not affect layers above.

Select a layer in the Layers palette. The adjustment layer will be positioned above the currently active layer. From the Layers palette pop-up choose New Adjustment Layer, or choose Layer > New > Adjustment.

You can restack adjustment layers as any other layer.

2 Choose a type from the Type pop-up menu. This automatically becomes the name for the layer. Enter a different name if desired. Set Opacity and Blending Mode at this stage if you want to. Click OK.

3 Depending on the type of adjustment layer you chose, the appropriate dialogue box opens. Create the settings you want to experiment with. OK the dialogue box.

4 The new adjustment layer appears in the Layers palette as the active layer. The settings you created are now applied to all layers below the adjustment layer.

5 Click the eye icon to hide/show the preview of the changes brought about by the adjustment layer settings. Double-click the adjustment layer to re-enter the appropriate adjustment dialogue box to make changes to the settings.

 The adjustment layer settings do not have a permanent effect on pixels until the layer is merged with other layers, or the image is flattened.

6 Drag the adjustment layer into the wastebasket if you want to discard the settings.

7 When you are ready to make the settings of the adjustment layer permanent, either use one of the Merge commands from the pop-up, or flatten the image.

Transparency

Layers have transparent areas where there are no pixels on the layer, allowing you to see through to pixels on other layers. Preserve Transparency enables you to control which pixels are affected when you paint on or edit a layer.

Hold down alt/Alt and click an eye icon to hide all layers other than the one you click on. Hold down alt/Alt and click the same eye icon again to show all layers.

To see transparent areas of a layer, hide all other layers by clicking on their eye icons. The transparent areas of the layer are represented by the checkerboard.

To work on a layer without affecting any of the transparent areas, select a layer, then make sure you select the Preserve Transparency option. In this example, painting with the Airbrush tool colours only existing pixels and does not affect the transparent areas of the layer where there are no pixels.

Transparent areas on a layer are indicated by the checkerboard pattern.

To colour existing pixels as well as the currently transparent areas of a layer, click the Preserve Transparency option to switch it off. Now when you paint on the layer or edit it in other ways, the transparent areas can be coloured – they are no longer protected from changes you make.

To select all pixels on a layer, hold down Command/Ctrl and click on the layer name in the Layers palette.

You can make pixels on individual layers semi-transparent by changing the Opacity setting for the layer.

New Layer Commands

The New Layer Via Cut (Command/Ctrl+Shift+J) and the New Layer Via Copy (Command/Ctrl+J) commands are essential options when creating layers. Use these commands to either cut or copy selected pixels to a new layer.

1   Start by making a selection. Then chose Layer > New > Layer Via Copy to create a new layer containing a copy of the selected pixels. The new layer is automatically named Layer 1, etc, depending on the number of layers already in the document.

Layer...	⇧⌘N
Adjustment Layer...	
Background	
Layer Via Copy	⌘J
Layer Via Cut	⇧⌘J

To move pixels on a layer, first make sure the layer is active, select the Move tool, position your cursor in the image window, then click and drag to move the pixels on the layer.

2   Make a selection, then choose New Layer Via Cut to cut the selected pixels to a new layer. Notice when you reposition the pixels on the new layer, the area on the Background layer from which they were cut is filled with the current background colour.

Layer Effects

Using the Layer Effects sub-menu, you can now create sophisticated layer effects such as soft shadows, bevelled and embossed edges, and inner and outer glows quickly and easily.

This example consists of 3 layers – a White background layer, a coloured circle on its own layer and a coloured triangle on another layer.

The following example uses Bevel and Emboss options to demonstrate the principles of using layer effects.

You can apply multiple Layer Effects to the same layer.

1 To apply a Layer Effect, click on a layer in the Layers palette to make it active. Choose Layer > Effects > Bevel & Emboss.

2 Use the Effect pop-up if you want to apply a different effect. Make sure the Apply option is selected and click the Preview option to see the effect applied in the image window with the default settings.

3 Adjust settings for the Highlight and Shadow edges of the effect. It is a good idea initially to leave the Modes set to Screen and Multiply respectively. Experiment with the Opacity sliders to create a more subtle effect.

4 Use the Style pop-up to choose a particular bevel or emboss type.

5 Enter a value in the Angle entry box to control the direction of the light source. Press and hold the black pop-up triangle to access the Angle disc if you prefer.

6 Use the Depth entry box or slider to adjust the height of the effect. Use the Blur entry box or slider to control the spread of the effect.

7 Select the Up/Down radio button to light the effect from above or below. OK the dialogue box when you are satisfied with the settings.

8 Notice in the Layers palette an 'f' symbol () on the layer, indicating that there is a layer effect applied to the layer. Whilst the 'f' symbol appears the layer effect remains editable.

Settings for the circle layer

Managing Layer Effects

Once you have created a layer effect you can continue to edit the effect and you can use a variety of commands from the Layer Effects sub-menu to manage the effects.

1 To edit the settings used to create a layer effect, make sure the appropriate layer is active, then use Layer > Effects to return to the layer effect you want to edit. Make changes to the settings, then OK the dialogue box. You can continue to adjust settings as long as the layer displays the layer effects icon.

Once you merge a layer with a layer effect applied to it, you can no longer adjust the layer effect settings.

2 To temporarily disable layer effects on all layers, not just the active layer, choose Layer > Effects > Hide All Effects. Repeat the process to show all layer effects.

3 To keep the angle of the light source constant if you are using multiple layer effects, choose Layer > Effects > Set Global Angle. Enter a value for the Angle in the Global Angle entry box. OK the dialogue box. Make sure you select the Use Global option when you create multiple layer effects in the Effects dialogue box.

4 To copy exact layer effect settings from one layer to another, first select a layer with a layer effect applied to it, then choose Copy Effects from the Effects sub-menu. Click on another layer in the Layers palette. Choose Paste Effects from the Effects sub-menu.

5 To permanently remove layer effects from a layer, make sure you select the appropriate layer, then choose Layer > Effects > Clear Effects.

6 Layer Effects automate procedures that in the past you had to perform yourself. Use the Create Layer command from the Effects sub-menu to separate the layer effect into the multiple layers that Photoshop has used to create the effect. This can be useful if you need to edit specific parts of the effect.

Transforming Layers

Once you have moved pixels to a new layer you can then transform the layer. Using Free Transform you can scale, rotate, distort, skew and create perspective effects.

You cannot transform the Background layer in an image.

1 Make sure the layer is active. Choose Edit > Free Transform. A bounding box with handles appears around the pixels on the layer.

2 To scale a layer, drag a handle on the bounding box. To scale in proportion, hold down Shift, then drag a corner handle.

To use Perspective and Distort transformations on a type layer, you must first render (convert to pixels) the type layer – Layer > Type > Render Layer.

3 To rotate a layer, position your cursor slightly outside the bounding box. The cursor changes to a bi-directional arrow. Drag in a circular direction. You can drag the point of origin marker to a new position to specify the point around which the rotation takes place.

4 To skew the layer, hold down Command/Ctrl+Shift, then drag either the centre top/bottom, or the centre left/right handle.

The Transform sub-menu (Edit > Transform) gives alternative options for transforming layers.

5 To reposition the layer, position your cursor inside the bounding box, then click and drag.

...cont'd

6   To create perspective, hold down
Command/Ctrl+alt/Alt+Shift, then
drag a corner handle.

7   To distort the layer, hold down
Command/Ctrl, then drag a corner handle.
This allows you to move corner handles
independently. Hold down Shift with the
Command/Ctrl key to constrain the
movement vertically or horizontally.

The advantage of Free Transform is that you can make multiple transformations, then either accept or discard the result.

8   To accept the transformation and remove the
Transformation bounding box, press Return/Enter, or
double-click inside the bounding box.

9   To revert to the original state without making changes, press
the Esc key.

Working with Type

Use the Type tools in Adobe Photoshop when the type needs to be an essential ingredient of the image. Although Photoshop offers considerable flexibility and control over type, ultimately applications such as QuarkXPress and Adobe PageMaker provide better all round type handling capabilities if the type is not integral to the image itself. For example, if you are simply layering a headline across an image you will have greater flexibiltiy creating the text in a page layout application.

When you create type it automatically appears on its own layer. You can keep type editable until you are ready to render it as pixels. Once type is rendered as pixels you can use further Photoshop commands on it that are unavailable when the type exists as an editable type layer.

The Type Mask tools allow you to create complex selections in the shape of type characters.

You can choose different alignments vertically and horizontally for type, you can rotate it, fill it with a gradient, pattern or image, create translucent type and much more.

Covers

Chapter Ten

Creating Type

You can choose the Type tool, or the Vertical Type tool to enter type. Type is automatically placed onto a type layer which is saved with the document. Additional type layers add to the overall size of the file. You can work with type layers as you would with any other layer.

1 To enter type, select either the Type or the Vertical Type tool. Position your cursor on the image where you want the type to start. Click. This sets the text insertion point. The Type Tool dialogue box appears.

2 Create settings for Font and Style, Size and Leading.

3 Click the Colour Box to specify a colour for the type. This opens the Colour picker dialogue box. (See page 66 for information on using the Colour Picker dialogue box.)

Use the Move tool to reposition a layer, including editable type layers.

4 Select the Preview option if you want to see a preview of the type in the image window. (This option is not available when working in Multichannel, Bitmap or Indexed Colour modes.)

5 Select an alignment option. For horizontal type the options are left aligned, centred, right aligned. For Vertical type the options are align top, align vertical centre, align bottom.

...cont'd

 When you create type in Multi-channel, Bitmap or Indexed Colour images, the type is placed directly onto the Background layer and it cannot be edited.

6 Click into the text entry window at the bottom of the dialogue box. Enter the text. The text appears formatted with the settings you have already created.

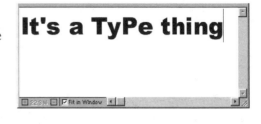

7 If you have selected the Preview option, you can drag the type preview in the image window to reposition the type.

8 Click OK or press Enter on the Numeric Keypad. The type is automatically placed on a new layer. The [T] icon indicates that this is a type layer and that the type layer is still editable.

Converting Type Layers

Convert a type layer to a standard layer when you no longer need to edit the text and its settings. The editable type is converted to pixels (rendered) which allows you the flexibility of using the full range of Photoshop commands and filters which are not available when type is on an editable type layer.

1 To convert type to a standard layer, click the type layer in the Layers palette.

2 Choose Layer > Type > Render Layer. The type layer becomes a standard layer and the [T] icon disappears to indicate this.

Type Settings

Font

Use the Font pop-up to choose from the list of fonts available on your system.

Size

Enter a value in the Size box for the size of your type. Use the Size pop-up to choose either points or pixels as the measurement system for type.

Leading

Leading controls the distance from one baseline of type to the next. Enter a leading value in the leading entry box. Leading is measured according to the size measurement option (points or pixels) that is selected. Photoshop applies a default leading value of 125% of the type size you have selected if you leave the leading box empty.

And the nights that have come between

Anti-Aliased

The anti-aliased option creates type with a slightly soft edge. It does this by blurring the pixels that form the edge of the type. Use this option to avoid unnecessary jagged edges in type, unless you are working with very small type.

Anti-aliased text has a softer edge, which is usually desirable. Text that is not anti-aliased can look jagged. The text opposite has been scaled to 200% to make the difference more prominent.

It is best not to use the Anti-Aliased option for type at very small sizes.

Kerning and Tracking

In the Type Tool dialogue box you can create settings for Kerning and Tracking. Auto Kern is on by default. Deselect the Auto Kern option if you do not want the built-in pair kerning table for the font to be automatically applied.

1   To kern character pairs, click between the characters in the text entry window to place the text insertion bar. Deselect the Auto Kern option. You can now enter a value in the Kerning entry box. Negative characters move characters closer together. Positive values move characters apart.

2   For Tracking, highlight a range of text you want to track. Enter a value in the Tracking entry box.

AWAY   Tracking = 84

AWAY   Tracking = -36

Baseline Shift

The Baseline Shift control allows you to move highlighted characters above or below their original baseline to create a variety of effects.

1   To baseline shift characters, in the text entry window, make sure you highlight the characters you want to shift.

It's a T^y P_e *thing*

2   Enter a positive value to baseline shift upwards, enter a negative value to baseline shift downward.

Editing and Selecting Type

It is important to keep type layers editable until you are satisfied that you will not need to make further changes to any of the settings available in the Type Tool dialogue box. When you are satisfied with your type settings, you can convert the editable Type layer to a standard layer. You will then be able to use the full range of Photoshop commands and filters on the layer – but you will no longer be able to edit the text or its settings.

There are some transformations and commands that you can apply to an editable type layer without first having to convert it to a standard layer. For example, you can use the Transformation commands available in the Edit menu (with the exception of Perspective and Distort). You can also use all the Layer Effects in the Layer menu.

Editing Type Settings

1 To edit a type layer, make sure that the Layers palette is showing. Double-click the name of the type layer.

2 In the text entry area, highlight the text you want to change. Make changes to the setting in the Type Tool dialogue box. Click OK.

3 Click the [+] or [-] zoom buttons to change the magnification of the text as it appears in the text entry area. This does not affect the text as it will appear in your image. Alternatively, select the Fit in Window option to automatically scale the text to fit in the text entry area.

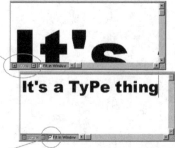

Selecting Text

Before you can make changes to settings for existing text, you must first select the range of text you want to change. You can now select either all the text on a type layer, or specific ranges of text in the text entry area of the Type Tool dialogue box to create mixed settings for type.

1   To select a specific range of text, click and drag across the text in the text entry area to highlight it.

2   Click in the text to place the text insertion point. This defines the start of the text you want to highlight. Move the cursor (do not press and drag), then hold down Shift and click to define the end of the range of text.

3   Double-click on a word to highlight one word.

4   Use Command/Ctrl+A to select all the text in the text entry area.

5   With the appropriate range of text highlighted you can then make changes to the settings. The changes you make apply to the highlighted text only.

Vertical and Rotated Type

Use the Vertical Type tool to create vertical type in the image. You can also create rotated vertical type.

To create vertical type, choose the Vertical Type tool. Click in the image window to specify the start position for the type. Create type settings as for standard type. Choose one of the Vertical Type Alignment options.

To change horizontal type into vertical type and vice versa, make sure the appropriate type layer is active, then choose Layer > Type > Vertical/ Horizontal.

Top

Centre

Bottom

2 To rotate vertical type, double-click the type layer to open the Type Tool dialogue box. Highlight the text you want to rotate. Select the Rotate option.

Type Mask Tools

In essence, use the Type Mask tools to create very complex selections – selections in the shape of type. This can be powerful and flexible when you want to show images through the shape of letterforms.

Because you do not get a preview of type settings in the image window when you use the Type Mask tool, create a standard type layer with the type settings you want before you use the Type Mask tool. Settings you create for the standard layer in the Type Tool dialogue box are remembered. Delete the standard type layer afterwards.

1 Select the Type Mask tool. Position your cursor on the image where you want the type to start. Click. This sets the text insertion point. The Type Tool dialogue box appears. Create settings for Font and Style, Size and Leading as for standard type.

2 OK the dialogue box. A type selection appears in the image window. With the Type Mask tool still selected, position your cursor inside the selection border, then click and drag to reposition the selection area if necessary. Notice that the Type Mask tool does not create a new layer.

3 You can now drag the selection to a new image window, create a new layer from the selection (see page 120), or use any commands that you would typically use on a selection.

Type and Layer Effects

Layer Effects can be applied to type layers whilst the type layer remains an editable-type layer.

1. To apply a Layer Effect to a type layer, first click on a type layer to make it active.

2. Choose a layer effect using the Effects sub-menu. Notice that the layer in the layers palette now has a [T] and an [f] icon indicating that it is an editable type layer with a layer effect applied. (See page 121 for information on working with layer effects. See page 132 for information on working with editable type layers.)

The editable type layer with its layer effect separated from the Background layer.

Yemen

Paths

An understanding of paths in Photoshop is essential for creating cut-outs for use in page layout applications such as QuarkXPress and Adobe PageMaker.

You can save paths with the image file in Photoshop format, convert paths into selections, or convert selections into paths. You can also export paths to Adobe Illustrator.

Covers

Chapter Eleven

Converting Selections to Paths

A quick and convenient technique for creating a path is to make a selection, convert the selection into a work path, and then into a path.

Use Window > Show Paths to show the Paths palette.

1 First make a selection using any of the selection tools. Then, use the Paths palette pop-up menu and choose Make Work Path, or click the Make Work Path icon.

You can only have one work path in the Paths palette at any one time. A work path is a temporary path only. For a path to be saved when you save your file, you must first save the path (see step 4, page 139).

2 The Make Work Path dialogue box appears if you use the Make Work Path command. Specify a tolerance value (from 0.5–10). (If you click the Make

Work Path icon, the last-used settings from the dialogue box are applied automatically.) The tolerance value controls how closely the path conforms to the selection. A low tolerance value creates a path that follows the selection tightly, but creates a greater number of points. A high tolerance value produces a path that follows the selection more loosely, but with fewer points.

3 OK the dialogue box. A work path appears in the Paths palette, along with a thumbnail of the path.

...cont'd

4 Choose Save Path from the pop-up menu if you want to save this path before making any adjustments to it. Enter a name. OK the dialogue box. The new path appears in the palette, replacing the work path.

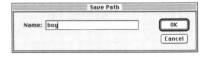

5 To hide the path, click in empty space in the Paths palette, or choose Turn Off Path from the pop-up menu. To show the path, click on the path name to select it. The path highlights.

Click in an empty area of the Paths palette to turn off the path, leaving the selection marquee only visible in the image window.

Converting Paths to Selections

You can also convert a path into a selection. This is useful when you want a very accurate selection.

To convert a path into a selection, click on the path in the Paths palette to highlight it. Then choose Make Selection from the pop-up menu, or click the Make Selection icon.

Creating Paths Using the Pen Tool

You can use the Pen tool to create paths. When you start to create a path it appears as a 'work path' in the Paths palette. A work path is only a temporary path.

The Pen tool creates anchor points which are connected by straight lines or curved segments. You can use the other tools in the Paths tool group to modify a path by adding, deleting or moving anchor points, and by changing the nature of the point, from smooth to corner and vice versa. You can also edit curved segments by dragging the Bezier direction points.

1 To create a path, double-click the Pen tool in the Toolbox to display the Pen Tool Options palette if it is not already showing. You can select the Rubber band option if you want to see a preview of the line segments as you draw.

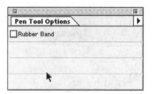

2 Position your cursor where you want to start drawing the path, then click, release the button, move the mouse and click again to create a straight line segment. Continue moving your cursor and clicking to create further straight line segments.

You can press the Delete key to delete the last anchor point. If you press Delete twice, you will delete the entire path.

3 Alternatively, you can click and drag to set an anchor point and create direction lines for a curve segment.

4 Then, release the button and move the cursor, and again click and drag to create the next anchor point with direction lines.

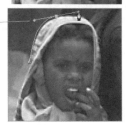

5 Continue in this way to create the path you want.

You can only have one work path in a file. It is a good idea to save the path and give it a name, so you do not delete it accidentally by creating another work path. See pages 138–139 for details on saving your work path.

6 Position the Pen tool cursor at the start point. Notice the cursor now has a small circle attached to it. Click to create a closed path. The path will appear in the Paths palette with the default title of Work Path.

7 To create an open path, follow the techniques outlined above, but instead of clicking back at the start point, click on the Pen tool in the Toolbox to finish the path. This is now an open path to which you could, for example, apply a stroke.

Showing and Selecting Paths and Points

Use the following techniques for selecting, deselecting and deleting paths.

1 To select a path, first you have to show it. To do this, click the path name in the Paths palette. The path now shows in the image window.

2 To select the path, select the Direct Selection tool (the hollow arrow). If necessary, click on the path to make it active. You will now see the curve and line segments together with the anchor points.

A selected anchor point is a solid square; a non-selected point is a hollow square.

3 Click on the anchor point of a curve segment to select the point and display the direction points.

4 To select and move an entire path, follow step 1 above, then hold down alt/Option (Mac) or Alt (Windows) and click on the path. Using the Direct Selection tool, position your cursor on an anchor point or curve segment, then click and drag to reposition the path. To deselect a path, click away from the path using the Direct Selection tool.

To improve the clarity of these screen shots, the path has been moved 1 pixel away from the edge of the image.

5 To delete a path, with a point or line segment of the path selected, press the Delete key twice. Alternatively, with the entire path selected, press the Delete key once. You can also drag the path name onto the Wastebasket icon in the Paths palette.

Adding, Deleting and Converting Points

You often need to add points and delete points on a path.

For a smooth point, when you drag one of the direction points, the other point balances it to maintain a smooth curve at the anchor point.

1 To add a point, make sure the path is selected, select the Add Point tool from the Pen Tool group, position your cursor on the path and then click. If you click on a curve segment you automatically get an anchor point with direction points. If you click on a straight line segment, you get just an anchor point.

2 To delete a point, make sure the path is selected, select the Delete Point tool, position your cursor on an existing anchor point, then click. The path redraws without the point.

A corner point is one which allows a sharp change of direction at the anchor point. Notice that for a corner point, when you drag one of the direction points, the other point is not affected. You have complete, independent control over each direction point.

3 To convert a smooth point into a corner point, select the Convert Anchor Point tool, position your cursor on a direction point, then click and drag. Use the Direct Selection tool to make any further changes to the direction points.

4 To convert anchor points on straight line segments into smooth points, select the Convert Anchor Point tool, position your cursor on the anchor point, then click and drag. Direction lines appear around the point. Use the Direct Selection tool to make any further changes to the points.

5 To convert a smooth point into a corner point without direction lines, select the Convert Anchor Point tool, then click on an anchor point.

Creating Corner Points

As you use the Pen tool to create paths, you can draw corner points as you go, in combination with straight line segments and smooth points. In many instances, a smooth point cannot create the shape of the path you want.

A corner point allows a sharp change of direction at the anchor point. In a corner point, the direction points can be manipulated independently. This is what makes them essential to create paths that require sharp changes of direction.

The paths in these screen shots have been moved one pixel away from the edge of the leaf so that they display more clearly. When you create a clipping path, it is best to position the path a pixel or so inside the shape you want to cut out, to avoid unwanted edge pixels being included. Unwanted edge pixels are sometimes referred to as 'edge tear'.

1 To draw a corner point, click and drag as you would to set a smooth point. Concentrate on getting the shape of the path coming into the point correct. Release the mouse button.

2 Position your cursor on the anchor point, hold down alt/Alt, then click and drag off the point. This converts the point to a corner point. You are now controlling the direction of the outgoing curve segment. As you drag the second direction point, notice that it no longer has any effect on the incoming direction point.

3 Move your cursor, then continue drawing either smooth or corner points.

Editing Points

Paths invariably need to be modified and fine-tuned to produce the result you require.

Select the Direct Selection tool to edit paths and points (see page 142, 'Showing and Selecting Paths and Points').

Select an anchor point and press the arrow keys to move the selected point in 1-pixel increments.

1 To edit a smooth point, make sure the path is selected, then click on the anchor point to select it. Direction points appear either side of the anchor point. Direction points control the shape and length of a curve segment.

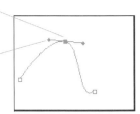

2 When you drag a direction point of a smooth anchor point, as you change the angle of one side, the other direction point moves to balance the point you are moving. This ensures the curve is always smooth through the anchor point.

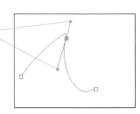

3 The further away from the anchor point you drag a direction point, the longer the associated curve segment becomes. As the curve segment is anchored at the anchor points at either end, this causes the curve segment to bow out more. Bring the direction point closer to the anchor point and the curve segment becomes shorter.

4 When you drag direction points on a corner anchor point, each moves totally independently of the other, allowing a sharp change of direction at the point.

Exporting Clipping Paths

Create a clipping path when you want to create transparent areas in an image that you intend to use in an application such as Adobe Illustrator or QuarkXPress.

A clipping path makes areas of the image outside the path transparent, allowing you to see past the outline of the image to the background on which the image is placed.

Flatness allows a PostScript printer to create less memory-intensive paths at output. If you use too high a flatness value, you get an approximate path that does not accurately conform to the path you created.

For high-resolution printing (1200–2400 dpi) a flatness value of 8 to 10 should be acceptable. Use a value of 1 to 3 for low resolution printing (300–600 dpi). Leave the field blank to use the printer's default setting.

1 Create a saved path (see page 138). If you have more than one path in the Paths palette, make sure you select the appropriate path. Use the pop-up palette to select Clipping Path.

2 Use the Path pop-up to specify a different path to make into a clipping path if necessary. Enter a flatness value.

3 When you have saved a clipping path, you need to save the file in EPS format for output. Choose File > Save As. In the Save As dialogue box, give the file a name and specify where you want to save it.

4 Choose Photoshop EPS from the Format pop-up. Click Save.

Remember to convert the file to an appropriate mode – e.g. CMYK – before you save the file in EPS format.

5 In the EPS Format dialogue box, specify a path that you want to be exported with the file as a clipping path. (You may

have more than one clipping path in an image, but you can only export one clipping path per file.) Set Preview and Encoding options (see page 48 in Chapter Three). OK the dialogue box.

Select a TIFF preview option if you intend to use the image on the Windows platform.

6 When you import the file into a QuarkXPress page, the clipping path hides areas of the image outside the clipping path. The second version of the same image on this Quark page has a white background and does not have a clipping path.

Exporting Paths to Adobe Illustrator

Exporting a path to Illustrator is useful when you want to place type along a path originated in Photoshop. The type can then be saved as an EPS file in Illustrator and placed back into Photoshop. This is useful because Photoshop does not have as much flexibility for creating type effects as Illustrator.

To export a path to Adobe Illustrator, choose File > Export > Paths to Illustrator. In the Export Paths dialogue box, change the name if necessary, but leave the automatically generated .ai extension to distinguish the file. If your Photoshop document has more than one saved path, use the Write pop-up to choose the path you want to export. Click Save.

2 Use File > Open in Adobe Illustrator to import the path and place type along it. Save the Illustrator file in EPS format.

3 Place the Illustrator EPS into the Photoshop document that you originally exported the path from. (See page 45, Chapter Three.)

4 Position the EPS bounding box, resize the EPS if necessary, then press Return/Enter to place the text from Illustrator onto a new layer.

Channels and Masks

The Channels palette stores colour information about an image and can also be used to store selections on a permanent basis.

Masks are created and used in a variety of ways in Photoshop. The basic principle of masks is that you use them to protect areas of an image from editing that you carry out on the unmasked areas of the image.

Use Quick Mask mode when you don't want to save the mask for future use. Layer masks control how different areas of pixels on a layer are hidden or revealed.

Covers

Chapter Twelve

Quick Mask Mode

In Quick Mask mode you create a 50% red, semi-transparent overlay. This overlay represents the protected area of the image. The overlay is similar in concept to a traditional rubylith mask. Quick Mask mode is particularly useful because you can see both the image and the mask as you create and fine-tune the mask.

You can make a rough selection first, then go into Quick Mask mode and edit the mask further if necessary.

1 To create a quick mask, click the Quick Mask Mode icon. Make sure that the default foreground and background colours are black and white respectively.

2 Show the Brushes palette and choose a brush size. Use a hard-edged brush for most control. Select a painting tool and drag across your image to 'paint' in the mask. Painting with black adds to the mask. Although you see through the 50% red mask, the pixels covered by the mask are completely protected.

Painting with grey or any other colour creates a semi-transparent or partial mask.

3 To remove areas from the mask you can use the Eraser tool, or paint with white.

4 When you are satisfied with your mask, click the Standard Mode button. This turns the areas of the image that were not part of your quick mask into a selection. You can now make changes to the selected areas (in this example the Blur filter has been applied), leaving the areas that were the quick mask unchanged.

The Channels Palette

The Channels palette (Window > Show Channels) shows a breakdown of the colour components that combine to make up the composite colour image that you work with most of the time on-screen.

You can change the display of channels from greyscale to the colour they represent by choosing File > Preferences > Display and Cursor. Select Colour Channels in Colour.

For example, in RGB mode, there are four channels – the composite image (all the other channels combined), and then a channel each for the red, green and blue colour components of the image. In CMYK mode, there are five channels.

Using the Channels palette you can be selective about which of the colour components in your image you change.

1 To switch to a specific channel, click the channel name in the Channels palette. The channel highlights to indicate that it is selected. The image window changes according to the channel you chose.

Indexed Colour mode, Greyscale mode and Bitmap mode all have only one channel.

2 You can view additional channels by clicking the eye icon for a channel. The image window changes, but your editing remains limited to the selected channel.

3 Click on the composite channel to return to normal image-editing view.

Saving and Loading Selections

Because you can only have one 'active' selection in an image at any one time, the facility to store a selection which can be reloaded later is vital, especially if the selection is complex and took some time to create. You save selections as an extra channel in the Channels palette. These extra channels are referred to as 'alpha channels'.

An alpha channel is an 8-bit greyscale channel, which means that every time you save a selection as a channel, you are adding to the file size of your image.

Saving Selections

1   To save a selection to a channel, make your selection on the image, then choose Select > Save Selection. The Save Selection dialogue box appears. Specify in which document you wish to save the channel. (You can save channels in another document to keep the file size of the current document as small as possible.) Leave the Channel pop-up on New. Enter a name for the channel. Click OK. Alternatively, make your selection and then click the Save Selection icon in the Channels palette.

You can only save an alpha channel with a picture in Photoshop, TIFF or PICT (RGB) file formats.

2   In the Channels palette, you will see an extra channel. This is the new 'alpha channel'. An alpha channel is a greyscale channel.

3   When you have saved a selection to an alpha channel you can freely deselect the selection in your image, as you can now reselect exactly the same area at any time using the alpha channel.

...cont'd

Loading Selections

Use the following process to re-select an area using the alpha channel:

1. To load a channel selection as a selection on the image, make sure the composite image is displayed. You can do this by clicking on the topmost channel name in the Channels palette. Then choose Select > Load Selection. The Load Selection dialogue box appears.

2. Use the Channel pop-up menu to specify which channel you want to load. Select an operation as appropriate. The operations allow you to control how the selection you are about to

load interacts with any existing selection in the image – adding to it, subtracting from it or intersecting with it. Click OK.

 When you are working in Quick Mask mode, you can turn the quick mask into an alpha channel by dragging the quick mask entry that appears in the Channels palette onto the New Channel icon.

3. Alternatively, using the Channels palette, drag the channel you want to load onto the Load Selection icon.

4. To delete a channel, drag the channel name onto the Wastebasket icon at the bottom of the palette.

Editing Alpha Channel Masks

You can display an alpha channel without loading it onto the image as a selection. You can then edit the mask by painting with black, white or grey.

1 To display an alpha channel, choose Windows > Show Channels to display the Channels palette. Click on the alpha channel you want to display. The channel name turns grey, and an eye icon in the left column of the palette indicates that this is the visible channel.

2 The image window changes from the composite view to a greyscale representation of the mask. The white area represents the selection and the black portions represent the protected areas.

3 To edit a selection channel, select a painting tool and brush size. Click the Default Colours icon if necessary, to change the foreground colour to black. Paint with black to remove areas from the selection. Paint with white on any black portion of the mask to add it to the selection.

HOT TIP
If you paint with grey you can create a semi-transparent mask.

BEWARE
Make sure you do not have a selection showing (marching ants) before you attempt to modify or edit the selection mask channel.

Another useful technique for editing a selection mask is to view a mask and image simultaneously by turning the alpha channel selection into a coloured mask (very much like using Quick Mask mode) and then reshaping the mask by painting with black, white or shades of grey.

...cont'd

1. To reshape a mask, make sure you don't have an active selection on your image. Click on the alpha channel in the Channels palette to select it. It highlights, and the eye icon shows on the left. The image window now displays the greyscale selection channel mask. Notice that the eye icon disappears from the Composite RGB channel as well as from the individual Red, Green and Blue channels.

Typically, when you edit masks, you will paint with black or white, with the mode set to Normal and an opacity of 100%. However, you can reduce the opacity or pressure setting in order to create a partial mask.

2. Click into the currently empty eye icon position for the Composite channel. The eye icon appears for the Composite channel, as well as in the individual Red, Green and Blue channels. The Composite channel now also shows in the image window. However, only the alpha channel is selected – indicated by the highlight.

Make sure that the eye icon for an alpha channel mask is not selected, then click the Composite channel when you want to return to the standard editing view.

3. The image window now changes in appearance. The selection mask area appears as normal, whilst the protected or masked portions of the image have a quick mask-type transparent film applied.

4. Select the paintbrush or pencil tool. Paint with white to remove areas of the image from the mask, in other words to enlarge the unmasked area. Paint with black to add portions of the image to the mask.

Layer Masks

Use layer masks to hide or reveal areas of a layer. A layer mask is extremely useful because you can use it to try out effects without actually changing the pixels on the layer. When you have achieved the result you want, you can apply the mask as a permanent change. If you are not satisfied, you can discard the mask without having permanently affected the pixels on the layer.

For information on creating layers, see Chapter Nine. For information on using filters, see Chapter Fourteen.

This example begins with an image with two layers. The background layer is the original scan; the other layer was created using the Render > Clouds filter.

1 To create a layer mask for the clouds layer, first click on the layer to make it active.

Choose Layer > Add Layer Mask > Reveal All. Reveal All means that all the pixels in the layer are visible. The Clouds layer now completely obscures the background layer.

You can only have one layer mask per layer.

2 In the Layers palette, the layer mask is active, indicated by the mask icon next to the eye icon. Click on the layer thumbnail to make the layer active (the paintbrush

icon indicates that you can now work directly on the layer). Click on the layer mask icon to continue editing the mask.

3 With the layer mask selected, make sure that the foreground colour is set to black. Choose a painting tool and start painting. Painting with black hides pixels on the clouds layer, revealing pixels on the Background layer.

4 Pixels on the clouds layer are not permanently erased when you paint with black. Paint with white to show pixels on the clouds layer – in effect hiding pixels on the background layer. (If you choose Layer > Add Layer Mask > Hide All, you start with the opposite scenario to the above. Now all the pixels on the clouds layer are hidden. Paint with white to reveal pixels on the clouds layer, paint with black to hide them.)

5 To temporarily switch off the Layer mask, choose Layer > Disable Mask, or hold down Shift, then click on the Layer Mask icon. To reactivate the mask, choose Layer > Enable Layer Mask, or hold down Shift, then click again on the Layer Mask icon.

6 To apply the layer mask as a permanent change, choose Layer > Remove Layer Mask, or drag the Layer Mask icon onto the Wastebasket icon in the bottom of the palette.

7 Click Apply. Once you apply a layer mask you lose the flexibility of making further changes – the effect is fixed. Click discard only if you want to delete the mask.

Channel and Quick Mask Options

The Channel Options dialogue box and the Quick Mask Options dialogue box allow you to control the colour of a mask and whether the protected or unprotected area of the image is coloured with the overlay.

1　To change channel options, double-click the alpha channel name. Alternatively, with the alpha channel selected, use the Channels pop-up menu to choose Channel Options.

2　In the Channel Options dialogue box you can enter a new name for the channel. You can also choose Selected Areas to reverse the way in which the colour will apply. In other words, masked (protected) areas will appear white, while the selection area (unprotected) will appear black.

3　To change the colour used to represent the masked (protected) area and its opacity, click the Colour box and choose a new colour from the colour picker.

4　To change the settings for a quick mask, double-click either the Quick Mask Mode icon or the Standard Mode icon, then make the appropriate changes in the dialogue box that appears.

Colour Correction Techniques

Colour correction involves making changes to the overall brightness and contrast in an image and also the colour balance to compensate for any tonal deficiencies and colour casts in the original scan.

You should bear in mind that although colour corrections can improve the overall appearance of an image, inevitably some colour values will be lost – certain pixels in the original scan that were different colours will end up remapped to the same colour.

Covers

Chapter Thirteen

The Brightness/Contrast Command

The Brightness/Contrast command provides the least complicated controls for changing overall brightness and contrast levels in an image. It does not allow you to make changes to individual colour channels.

1   To change brightness and contrast, choose Image > Adjust > Brightness/Contrast.

2   Drag the Brightness and Contrast sliders to the right or left, or enter a value in the entry boxes (-100 to +100). OK the dialogue box.

3   If you are making adjustments to a selection, click the Preview button to see, on-screen, the result of the settings you choose.

The Auto Levels Command

Auto Levels allows you to adjust brightness and contrast automatically. Auto Levels examines each colour channel independently and changes the darkest pixels to black and the lightest pixels to white, then redistributes the remaining shades of grey between these two points.

Auto Levels works best on images that have a reasonably even distribution of tonal values throughout the image, as it redistributes pixels based on white and black points, with a tendency to increase contrast. This generally produces good results, but Auto Levels does not allow the precision of manual adjustments that you can make using the Levels and Curves dialogue boxes.

1   To apply Auto Levels to an image, choose Image > Adjust > Auto Levels. (Use Edit > Undo if you do not like the result.)

2   You can also use the Auto Levels command from within the Levels and Curves dialogue boxes. Click the Auto button.

The Levels Dialogue Box

Use the Levels dialogue box (Image > Adjust > Levels) to adjust the tonal balance for colour and greyscale images. You can adjust highlight, shadow and midtone ranges for a selection or an entire image, or you can make changes to individual channels only.

Input Levels

The Input Level sliders and entry boxes allow you to improve the contrast in a 'flat' image.

 The most flexible way of working with Levels, Curves and Colour Balance is to set up Adjustment layers. Adjustment layers allow you to readjust settings in the respective dialogue boxes until you are satisfied with the result. (See page 117.)

1 Use the Channel pop-up menu to select a channel. If you do not select an individual channel, you work on the composite image and affect all channels.

2 To darken an image, drag the solid black slider to the right. Alternatively, enter an appropriate value in the leftmost Input Levels entry box. This maps or clips pixels to black. For example, if you drag the black slider to 15, all pixels with an original value between 0 and 15 become black. The result is a darker image.

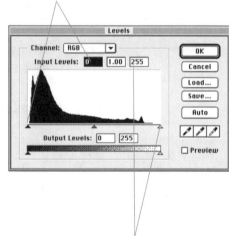

Dragging either or both the black or white sliders inwards has the effect of increasing contrast in the image.

3 To lighten an image, drag the hollow, white Input Levels slider to the left. Alternatively, enter an appropriate value in the rightmost Input Levels entry box. The result is to map or clip pixels to white. For example, if you drag the white slider to 245, all pixels with an original value between 245 and 255 become white. The result is a lighter image.

...cont'd

Gamma

The grey triangle and the middle Input Levels entry box control the Gamma value in the image. The Gamma value is the brightness level of mid-grey pixels in the image.

 When you OK the Levels dialogue box, you can use Edit > Undo/Redo a number of times to evaluate the changes.

1 To lighten midtones, drag the grey slider to the left, or increase the Gamma value in the Input Levels entry box above the default setting of 1.00.

2 To darken midtones, drag the grey slider to the right, or decrease the Gamma value in the Input Levels entry box.

Output Levels

You can use the Output Levels entry boxes or sliders to decrease the amount of contrast in an image.

1 Drag the black Output Levels slider to the right to lighten the image and reduce the contrast.

 See page 161 for an explanation of Auto Levels and the Auto button.

2 Drag the white Output Levels slider to the left to darken the image and reduce the contrast.

The Curves Dialogue Box

The Curves dialogue box (Image > Adjust > Curves) offers the most versatile set of controls for making tonal adjustments in an image. The central brightness graph in the dialogue box displays the original and adjusted brightness values for pixels in the image. The graph is a straight line from 0 (black) to 255 (white), before any adjustments are made – input and output values for pixels are the same.

You should be careful not to click on the brightness bar at the bottom of the Curves dialogue box accidentally.

The horizontal axis of the graph represents the original or input values, the vertical axis represents the output or adjusted values. By adjusting the brightness curve, you are remapping the brightness values of pixels in the image.

The default brightness bar starts black and graduates to white. In this state, the brightness curve indicates the brightness values of colours in the image; the brightness curve starts at O, for black, and moves to 255, for white.

1 To add a point to the curve, select the Point tool. (This is the default selection.) Click on the curve. (You can add up to fifteen points.) Drag the point(s) around to edit the curve. Alternatively, click at a point in the graph and the curve will change according to where you clicked.

2 To delete a point, click on a point to select it, then press the Delete/Backspace key. You can also drag it outside the Brightness graph.

3 To lighten an image, select the Point tool, position your cursor near the midpoint of the graph, then click to place a new point. Click and drag this point upwards.

...cont'd

Hold down alt/Alt, then click on the Reset button (previously Cancel) to restore the original settings in the dialogue box.

4 To darken an image, select the Point tool, position your cursor near the midpoint of the graph, then click to place a point. Drag the point downwards.

5 To increase the contrast in an image, place a point at roughly the ¼ tone part of the graph and drag this upwards to lighten the highlights. Next, place a point at roughly the ¾ tone part of the graph. Drag this downward to darken the shadow areas. The result is to increase the contrast in the image by lightening the highlights and darkening the shadows, whilst leaving the midtones more or less untouched.

6 Reverse the setting in step 5 to decrease the contrast in an image.

7 To limit changes to the midtones and highlights, click on the graph to place a point at the ¾ tones. Place a point at the ¼ tones and drag this upwards. Reverse this procedure to change midtones and shadows without affecting highlights.

The Colour Balance Dialogue Box

Like the Brightness/Contrast command, the Colour Balance dialogue box provides general controls for correcting an overall colour cast in an image. As such, it provides the least complex method of colour correction.

The Colour Balance dialogue box works on the principle of complimentary colours. If there is too much cyan in an image, you drag the Cyan–Red slider towards red to remove the cyan colour cast. If there is too much magenta, drag the Magenta–Green slider towards green.

Work on the composite view of an image when using the Colour Balance dialogue box.

| To adjust the colour balance of an image, choose Image > Adjust > Colour Balance. Click the Shadow, Midtone or Highlights radio button to specify the tonal range to which you want to make changes.

2 Drag the colour sliders to reduce/increase the amount of a colour in the image.

Preserve Luminosity
Select this option to prevent brightness values from changing as you change colour levels. This helps maintain the overall colour balance in the image.

Filters

Photoshop ships with more than 95 filters as standard. Filters add enormous creative flexibility and potential to image-manipulation, and they are well worth experimenting with.

You can use filters across an entire image, or you can apply them to selections to limit the results to specific areas. Filters cannot be applied to images in Bitmap or Indexed Colour mode.

Covers

Chapter Fourteen

Filter Controls

Many of the filters have standard controls, which are explained below.

2 Click and drag on the image in the Preview window to scroll around to preview different parts of the image. Alternatively, with the filter dialogue box active, position your cursor in the main image window – the cursor becomes a hollow box – then click to set the view in the Preview window.

1 Click the Preview check box to see the effect of your settings previewed in the main image window, as well as in the Preview window inside the filter dialogue box.

If you have the Preview box checked, click and hold on the Preview window inside the filter dialogue box to see the image without the filter settings applied.

3 Click the '+' or '–' buttons to zoom in or out on areas of the image. You can also use the Command + Spacebar (Mac) or Ctrl + Spacebar (Windows) keyboard shortcuts within the Preview window or the image window.

4 Hold down alt/Alt and click the Reset button (previously Cancel) to revert to the original settings in the dialogue box.

5 After you OK a filter dialogue box, use Command + F (Mac) or Ctrl + F (Windows) to reapply the last-used filter and its settings.

A line flashing under the Preview check box means that Photoshop is still rendering the new settings.

Unsharp Mask and Sharpen Filters

These filters allow you to enhance the detail of your images.

Unsharp Mask

This is a powerful function which can help you to sharpen blurry images in specific areas. For example, if you rotate an image, or change the dimensions or resolution of the image, it may blur due to any interpolation that Photoshop applies. This can also happen when you convert from RGB to CMYK. Where the Unsharp Mask filter finds edges (areas where there is a high degree of contrast), it increases the contrast between adjacent pixels. The result is to create an apparent improvement in the focus of the image.

1 To use Unsharp Mask to sharpen an image, choose Filter > Sharpen > Unsharp mask. The Unsharp Mask dialogue box appears.

2 Adjust settings for Amount, Radius and Threshold. Click OK or press Return/Enter.

Amount – Use this to control the amount of sharpening applied to the edges (minimum = 1, maximum = 500). The picture will become pixellated if the amount is too high.

Values below 50% produce subtle effects; values between 50% and 250% produce moderate results, while values between 300% and 500% produce dramatic, exaggerated results.

The settings for Radius and Threshold need to be taken into account when setting the amount value (see the next page).

Radius – Radius controls the depth of pixels along the high-contrast edges that are changed.

A low radius value restricts the impact of the filter; higher values distribute the impact. Radius values of 2.0 or lower usually produce acceptable sharpening.

Threshold – Sets a level for the minimum amount of contrast between pixels an area must have before it will be modified. The Threshold value is the difference between two adjacent pixels – as measured in brightness levels – that must occur for Photoshop to recognise them as an edge.

 On high-resolution images, use a Threshold value of 10 or higher to apply the sharpening effect to specific areas only.

High threshold values limit changes to areas where there is a high degree of colour difference. Use low values to apply the filter more generally throughout the image.

Sharpen and Sharpen More

Use the Sharpen and Sharpen More filters when an image becomes blurred after resampling. Both filters work by increasing contrast between adjacent pixels throughout the image or selection. Sharpen More has a more pronounced effect than Sharpen.

Sharpen Edges

This filter has a more specific effect, applying sharpening along high-contrast edges. In effect, it has a less global impact on a selection or image than Sharpen and Sharpen More.

Blur Filters

The Blur filters reduce the contrast between adjacent pixels along edges where considerable colour shifts occur, to create a softening, defocusing effect. Blurring produces the opposite effect to sharpening – which increases the contrast between adjacent pixels.

Blur More produces an effect roughly 3 times stronger than the Blur filter.

'Blur' and 'Blur More' blur a selection in preset amounts offering only a limited degree of control. For greater control when blurring you can use the Gaussian Blur option, which blurs according to a bell-shaped Gaussian distribution curve.

To Blur a Layer or Selection

Create a selection if you want to limit the effect of the Blur filter to a specific area of your image. Choose Filter > Blur > Blur, or Filter > Blur > Blur More.

Motion Blur

You can use Motion Blur to create the effect of a moving subject or camera.

1 To create a motion blur, make a selection, if required. Choose Filter > Blur > Motion Blur.

Angle = 0,
Distance = 12

2 Enter a value in the Angle box, or drag the Angle indicator to specify the angle or direction of the blur.

Enter a value in the Distance entry box to specify the distance in pixels for the blur effect. OK the dialogue box.

Angle = -45,
Distance = 12

Angle = -53,
Distance = 26

Radial Blur

Radial Blur creates the effect of zooming in as you take a picture.

1 To create a radial blur, make a selection if required. Choose Filter > Blur > Radial Blur.

 If you are working on a layer, make sure that Preserve Transparency is deselected for the blur to take effect.

2 Select a Blur Method and Quality, and specify an Amount (0–100). Click and drag in the Blur Centre window to specify the centre point for the zoom or spin effect. OK the dialogue box.

Amount – This value determines the distance pixels are moved to create the blur effect. Higher values produce more intense effects.

Zoom – Choose Zoom to create a zoom-like blurring effect.

Spin – Spin rotates and blurs pixels around a central point.

Quality – Good and Best produce better, smoother results due to the interpolation methods used, but take longer.

Noise Filters

Add Noise

The Add Noise filter randomly distributes high-contrast pixels in an image, creating a grainy effect.

> To add noise, create a selection, or work on the entire image. Choose Filter > Noise > Add Noise. Specify Amount, Distribution and Monochromatic options.

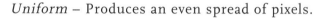

Amount – Determines the degree to which pixels are changed from their original colour. Enter a number from 1–999.

Uniform – Produces an even spread of pixels.

Gaussian – Produces a more dramatic result.

Monochromatic – Choose Monochromatic to distribute greyscale dots.

You can use Add Noise to reduce banding in graduated fills.

Add Noise is a good way to begin creating textured backgrounds.

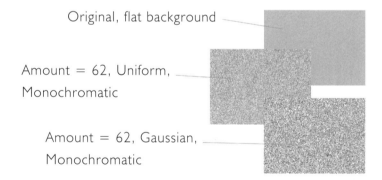

Original, flat background

Amount = 62, Uniform, Monochromatic

Amount = 62, Gaussian, Monochromatic

Dust & Scratches

Use the Dust & Scratches filter to remove small imperfections and blemishes in a scan caused by dust, scratches. The degree of success you have with this filter depends very much on the image or selection to which you apply it.

Radius and Threshold settings are interdependent, and both are taken into account before changes are made.

| To remove dust and scratches, create a selection or work on the entire image. Choose Filters > Noise > Dust & Scratches. Specify Radius and Threshold settings. Click OK.

Radius – Determines how small a blemish must be for it to be worked upon by the filter. For example, at a radius of 3 pixels, the Dust & Scratches filter will not attempt to make changes to imperfections above this size.

Threshold – Specifies the minimum amount of contrast between pixels there must be before changes are made.

Despeckle Filter

This produces the opposite effect to Add Noise, smoothing and blurring the image, but having little effect on edges.

Median Filter

The Median filter also removes noise from a poor-quality scan. It works by averaging the colour of adjacent pixels in an image.

| To use the Median filter, create a selection, or work on the entire image. Choose Filter > Noise > Median. Specify a Radius value (1–16). OK the dialogue box.

Filter Samples

The following examples of filters provide only a sample of the complete range of filters available in the Filter menu.

 Use Command + F (Mac) or Ctrl + F (Windows) to reapply the last-used filter and settings.

Original

Artistic

Coloured Pencil   Cut Out

Dry Brush   Film Grain

 It is well worth making a copy of your image to work on before you start experimenting with filters.

Brush Strokes

Accented   Angled
Edges   Strokes

Cross Hatch   Dark Strokes

Distort

Diffuse Glow   Glass

Ocean Ripple   Pinch

 Choose Filter > Fade... to reduce the effect of a filter on an image.

Pixellate

Colour
Halftone   Crystallise

Facet   Fragment

Render

Difference
Clouds   Clouds

Lens Flare   Lighting Effects

Original

Sketch

Bas Relief   Chalk and Charcoal

Charcoal   Chrome

Stylise

Diffuse   Emboss

Extrude   Find Edges

Texture

Craquelure   Grain

Mosaic Tiles   Patchwork

Other

Custom   High Pass

Maximum   Minimum

Artistic

Fresco   Neon Glow

Paint Daubs   Palette Knife

Web and Multimedia Images

The success of the World Wide Web is in no small part due to its ability to include images in HTML pages. This section looks at some of the considerations for using different image types effectively in formats suited to the environment of the WWW. It also covers using images for multimedia work.

Balancing file size and image quality is a primary concern when creating images for Web and multimedia use. Generally, the smaller the file size, the quicker the image will load and display on screen. The following techniques examine ways of reducing file size without losing too much image quality.

An image resolution of 72 ppi is usually satisfactory for images intended for screen-based presentations.

Covers

Chapter Fifteen

Indexed Colour Mode

Indexed Colour mode is an important factor in the preparation of images for use on the World Wide Web and in multimedia applications. Some multimedia animation applications only support 8-bit colour.

Indexed Colour mode provides an efficient method for reducing the size of a colour image. When you work on RGB colour images in Photoshop, these are typically 24-bit images, capable of displaying over 16 million colours. Indexed Colour Mode converts images to single channel, 8-bit images, capable of displaying a maximum of 256 colours.

1 To convert an RGB colour image to Indexed Colour mode, choose Image > Mode > Indexed Colour.

2 Use the Palette pop-up to specify a colour palette which controls and limits the colours that will be used in the image.

 When you save a file with an image preview, you increase the size of the file. To save files without a preview, select File > Preferences > Saving Files > Never Save (in the Image Previews pop-up menu).

Exact
If the image you are converting already has fewer than 256 colours, Exact is the default. The actual number of colours is indicated in the Colours entry box. You cannot dither an exact palette.

System Palettes
This is the standard, 8-bit system palette of either the Macintosh or Windows system.

Web

This is a palette reduced to 216 colours. Use this palette to achieve consistency across different platforms and when you want to use more than one image on the same Web page. Images which are based on different colour palettes can look artificial when seen side by side.

Uniform

This palette is based on a uniform sampling of colours from the colour spectrum.

 Make a selection before you convert to Indexed Colour mode, to weight the colour table towards the colours that occur in the selection.

Adaptive

This palette is built around the colours that actually occur in an image. For individual images, it gives better results than Web, as the colour table is created by sampling colours from the most frequently occurring areas of the colour spectrum in the image.

Custom

This option takes you into the Colour Table dialogue box and allows you to create your own custom colour table.

Previous

Previous is only available after you have converted an image using either Adaptive or Custom methods. It uses exactly the same palette as created by the previous conversion.

Don't use dithering for images you intend to use on the Web. Dithering mixes available colours to simulate colours that are not actually in the colour palette. This can produce a speckled, mottled result.

1 You can specify an exact number of colours for an Indexed Colour image if you don't want the maximum 256 steps. You can also specify a reduced bit-depth from the Colour Depth pop-up to further reduce the file size of the image.

| 3 bits/pixel |
| 4 bits/pixel |
| 5 bits/pixel |
| 6 bits/pixel |
| 7 bits/pixel |
| • 8 bits/pixel |
| Other |

2 Select a dither option if you want the colours available in the colour palette to be mixed in the image, to simulate colours that are not actually in the palette. (Pattern is available only when using a System palette.) OK the dialogue box.

| • None |
| Diffusion |
| Pattern |

Saving Indexed Colour Images as GIFs

When you have converted an image to Indexed Colour mode, you can then proceed to save the image in GIF format.

This technique works best for flat coloured images such as logos. For photographic type images with subtle colour transitions, JPEG is a better method of preparing images for the World Wide Web.

You cannot specify transparency with this method. See page 181 for creating GIFs with transparent areas.

Avoid using GIF format if your image contains a gradient. Use JPEG format instead (see page 186).

1 To save the image in GIF format, choose File > Save As. Specify CompuServe GIF from the Format pop-up menu. Specify a location for saving the file and enter a name. Make sure you use the '.gif' extension. OK the dialogue box.

```
Save this document as:
LTLogo.gif
Format:  CompuServe GIF  ▼
```

2 Click the Interlaced option in the GIF Options dialogue box if you want a low-resolution image to download first, followed by progressively more image information as it becomes available from the Web server.

```
GIF Options
Row Order
⦿ Normal          OK
○ Interlaced      Cancel
```

Exporting Indexed Colour Images as GIFs

 The disadvantage of using this method is that you cannot control or reduce the number of colours in the final GIF.

If you have an Indexed Colour image which you want to convert to a GIF image with transparent areas, you have to export it rather than use the method on the previous page. In this case it's a simple logo which is semi-transparent and has lots of white around it.

| Choose File > Export > GIF89a Export.

2 To create transparent areas in the image, select the Eyedropper + tool. Either click in the preview to specify transparency, or click the swatch you want to be the transparent colour.

 Hold down Alt/ Option (Mac) or Alt (Windows) and click the Reset button to restore the original settings.

3 The Transparency Index Colour box controls the transparent colour. The default is the equivalent of Netscape Navigator's default grey background.

4 Click the Transparency Index Colour box if you want to specify a different colour to be used to represent transparent areas. In the Colour Picker, choose a new colour then OK the dialogue box.

5 Select the Interlaced option to specify that the image downloads a low-resolution version which is progressively built up as more information is received from the Web server.

6 OK the dialogue box when you are satisfied, and make sure you save the file with the '.gif' extension.

Exporting RGB Images in GIF Format

You can use layers to create transparent areas in GIF images, when you export an RGB image in GIF format.

The advantages of converting an RGB image to GIF format are that you can feather the selection you move to a new layer, and that you also have the option to further reduce the number of colours in the GIF file you export.

1 Select the areas of your image that you want to display when the image is downloaded as part of an HTML file.

2 Create a new layer (see Chapter Nine, 'Layers'), then copy the selection to the new, transparent layer.

3 Hide the other layers in the file. (Click on the eye icon in the Layers palette to hide a layer.)

Reducing the number of colours in an image reduces its file size, depending on the size of the image and the original colour content, but you can only specify a reduced number of colours when you export an RGB image to GIF format.

4 Choose File > Export > GIF89a Export.

5 To display transparent areas with a solid colour, you can leave the Transparency Index Colour box as it is. This is the default Web browser grey background colour. Alternatively, click the Transparency Index Colour box and choose a new colour for the transparent areas.

6 Select a palette from the pop-up menu.

7 Use the Preview button to evaluate the result of reducing the number of colours on quality. OK the Preview dialogue box. Change the number of colours if necessary.

8 Select the Interlaced option to specify that the image downloads a low-resolution version which is progressively built up as more information is received from the server.

9 OK the dialogue box to save the file. Make sure you leave the .gif extension in place.

Greyscale Images for the Web

The best way to prepare greyscale images for the World Wide Web is to convert them to RGB mode first. Then, when you export in GIF format, you will be able to reduce the number of colours to reduce file size and speed up download times.

1 Open a greyscale image. Choose Image > Mode > RGB Colour. Then choose File > Export > GIF 89a. This converts the image to indexed colour.

2 See 'Exporting RGB Images in GIF Format' on the previous two pages for how to use the GIF 89a Export settings.

3 You can dramatically reduce the number of colours in a greyscale image exported as a GIF without losing too much quality. Click the Preview button if you want to see a preview of the image and the colour table, to check that the quality of the image is acceptable.

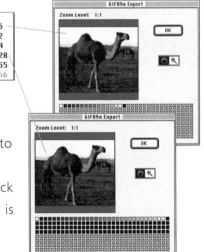

JPEG Format for Web Images

JPEG is a compression format, which is why it is useful when preparing images for the World Wide Web. Browsers such as Netscape Navigator and Internet Explorer both support the JPEG format. Use JPEG when you are working with photographic-type images, and when preserving colour detail and quality in the image are more important than download time considerations. JPEG does not allow transparency, and file sizes may be larger than for images exported in GIF format, depending on the compression level you choose.

For a general introduction to JPEG format, see page 49.

However, you should save images with gradients in JPEG format. When working with gradients, JPEG format produces smaller file sizes than GIFs with an Adaptive palette.

1 To save an image in JPEG format, choose File > Save As. Specify a location, enter a name, then choose JPEG from the Formats pop-up. OK the dialogue box.

JPEG is most suited to compressing continuous-tone images (images in which the distinction between immediately neighbouring pixels is slight). JPEG is not the best format for saving flat colour images.

2 Use the Quality pop-up to specify the amount of compression, or drag the slider. 'Maximum' gives best quality, retaining most of the detail in the image, but least compression. 'Low' gives lowest image quality, but maximum compression.

3 For Format Options, choose Baseline Optimised to optimise the colour quality of the image.

4 Select Progressive and enter a number for Scans. The image will download in a series of passes which add detail to the image progressively until it is completely displayed.

5 Click OK to export the file.

Index